STEPHEN WYNN was born in Leeds in 195
officer since 1983, specializing twice durii
nine years as a member of a specialist firearms unit and, for the last
eleven years, as youth liaison officer working to keep youngsters
away from criminality. For the past seven years he has been married
to Tanya, his partner and best friend, and they live in Essex with
four very lively German Shepherd dogs. Stephen has three children:
Luke aged 23 and Ross aged 22 — both currently serving in the
military — and Aimee, who is aged 10. Stephen's main hobbies are
football (he supports Leeds United Football Club) and writing (he
has several fictional projects in various stages of development). He
describes himself as a straightforward and uncomplicated person.

TWO SONS IN A WAR ZONE

AFGHANISTAN: THE TRUE STORY OF A FATHER'S CONFLICT

Stephen Wynn

CLAIRVIEW

Clairview Books
Hillside House, The Square
Forest Row, East Sussex RH18 5ES

www.clairviewbooks.com

Published by Clairview 2010

A catalogue record for this book is available from the British Library

ISBN 978 1 905570 24 9

Cover by Andrew Morgan Design
Typeset by DP Photosetting, Neath, West Glamorgan
Printed and bound in Malta by Gutenberg Press

® **Mixed Sources**
Product group from well-managed
forests, and other controlled sources
www.fsc.org Cert no. TT-CoC-002424
FSC © 1996 Forest Stewardship Council

The paper used for this book is FSC-certified and
totally chlorine-free. FSC (the Forest Stewardship
Council) is an international network to promote
responsible management of the world's forests.

Contents

Acronyms

BRF	Brigade Recce Force
CID	Criminal Investigation Department
CTC	Commando Training Centre
ECM	Electronic countermeasure
FMOs	Force Medical Officers
FOB	Forward Operating Base
FSU	Force Support Unit
IED	Improvised Explosive Device
ISAF	International Security Assistance Force
KAF	Kandahar Air Field
MC	Military Cross
MOD	Ministry of Defence
PRMC	Potential Royal Marine Course
R & R	Rest and Recuperation
RPG	Rocket Propelled Grenade
SFSG	Special Forces Support Group
VCP	Vehicle Check Point

This book is dedicated to the memory of my late mother, Angela Wynn, who passed away on 4 January 2010, two days shy of her 84th birthday. She was a truly remarkable woman and a wonderful mother to myself and my sister Teresa.

She only discovered the joy of reading in her early 70s and was so looking forward to reading this book, written by her son and about her grandsons. Sadly she never got to read it, although if heaven has a copy in its library, I'm sure she will.

Acknowledgements

I want to acknowledge and give due credit to the following people for their time, effort, assistance and friendship through the ordeal this book records.

Firstly, my two sons, Luke and Ross, without whom this book would never have been written. Guys, I love you both very much indeed. May your God be with you and keep you safe always.

Laura Anderson: Thank you for the positive comments and advice that you gave me at the beginning when this book was still very much a dream. Your honesty was much appreciated.

Humphrey Price, for his advice and support with the book and the direction that he believed it should take.

Matthew Barton, for his sensible and sensitive editing.

Ray Williams, MBE: Thanks for your support, sense of humour and concern along the way. It was a big help. You now know an author . . .

Darren Griffin, BBATIT — which stands for *Bitten By A Tiger in Thailand*: Thanks for being a good mate. We have had some good laughs along the way.

My publisher Sevak Gulbekian, for having enough belief in my story to publish this book. A true gentleman.

My daughter Aimee: I love you very much and I will write the 'But Mum' books one day . . .

And finally, Tanya, my loving wife: Thank you for your continual support and love — and I don't just mean while writing this book. You are one of life's really nice, genuine, caring people who bring out the best in everybody you touch. With you, life is a stroll in the park, and there's no such thing as a bad day. I love you very much and always will.

Prologue

This book started out as a diary of one year in my life, as a mechanism for coping with the passion, distress and rage I felt while my sons were on active service in Afghanistan. It helped give me back some control over the impotent situation I found myself in, which was not of my own making.

I'm not one to bottle up what's inside me, and never have been. Nor am I someone who sits about and examines every feeling, then bores everyone else rigid by talking about it. I was brought up to deal with things myself. As a man, I learned, you went through something, and found some way to express yourself – when I was younger, football was my outlet – and didn't moan on about it to all and sundry.

Well this was different. I promised myself that I would not hide my feelings from anyone. I would not be wilfully ignorant of the risks my sons were facing out there. Though they were men, to me they were still boys, and they would be facing boys like themselves – boys, and men younger than me, who would shoot at them. Knowing this, how would I get through a single day? Would I have to bottle up how I felt? No, I'd be open, and honest. I wasn't planning to cry openly, but I was ready to be upfront about my feelings, not waste energy hiding them.

I flattened myself against the wall, my hands sweaty as I gripped the stock of my Heckler & Koch MP5 semi-automatic carbine. I could feel my heart beating hard in my chest as I stood still, waiting to hear something – any indication that I'd been spotted. After a moment I felt safe to move again. I slid along the bricks, reaching the corner which – slowly, very slowly – I peered round. Ahead, almost directly in front of me and no more than 40 metres away, the dark windows of the house we'd been told to target seemed like eyes boring into me, waiting to see what I would do next. Any second now and I would have to move. The only chance I had was to be ready when whoever was in there took aim at me. I pulled my head back round the corner and took a deep breath, needing to be completely focused.

I crouched down slowly until I had one knee on the ground, my leg bent behind it so that I could steady myself into the perfect firing position before I shot. It had been drummed into us: get yourself into a triangular position, it's the most stable there is, one leg down, the other up, your upper body resting against a solid surface – then ready yourself to shoot. This is fine, assuming of course that you're not yourself a target at the same time. So far, and as far as I knew, I wasn't.

The surrounding ground was dry now and dusty as I knelt there; I had been moving slowly to prevent any dust rising up, not because it might identify my position, but so it wouldn't make me sneeze – a giveaway. The whole place was tatty but clean; there was nothing lying about in the roadway that shouldn't be there.

I checked the ground ahead of me for any sign of sticks or anything else that might make a noise when I leaned round the corner again. Stones would also be painful if I knelt on one of them unexpectedly. I settled more tightly into my position, holding it while I waited for the inevitable moment to come. I didn't need to look to my right or left to know that my colleagues were there alongside me, also in safe hiding positions, also readying themselves for the attack. They too had their targets; they too would wait until called upon to return fire. If I wanted, or needed to, I could have spoken with them, but we'd been told to be silent in our assault on the position, so silent we were.

We'd also been told to be careful. This was someone's home, after all, not a base for soldiers, and not everyone we saw would be a target – they might easily be a child, a woman, or maybe an old man. We would have to make our minds up in moments briefer than seconds whether or not to open fire. If we got this wrong and shot an innocent person, we'd not only have to be able to justify our actions and deal with the immediate consequences but also live with it for the rest of our lives.

I carefully lifted my gun to my shoulder, pressing the stock against *myself hard and resting my cheek on the cold metal so that I could look down the sights. There at the end was the window, its darkness like a presence calling me. I felt my finger twitch on the trigger, an indication, like the hairs standing up on the back of my neck, that something was about to happen. And then – faster than I could fully register – something appeared in the window, and instinctively I . . .*

. . . jerked awake. I was back, in my own bed, far away from that place and time. I knew why I was thinking about it now, why the place had haunted my recent dreams. I had been there some years before; but my son Ross was there only a few weeks back. And tomorrow – today, probably – Ross was off to a place where that kind of tense confrontation would be for real, not an exercise. He was going to Afghanistan, and there was nothing I could do to help him through it.

I lay in my bed, full of confused and confusing feelings. The dream was of my time in the training village. I had wanted to know what it would be like for him, over there in Helmand Province, and so in my sleep I'd tried to put myself in his shoes. What would he go through? How would he cope? I closed my eyes again and daydreamed about the rapid response training I'd done, only this time I imagined it was warmer – an alien heat – that smelt differently, and was noisier; and the people alongside me were in army, not police uniforms.

It didn't work. I had no idea what Ross would go through, even though I felt I knew something about it from my own experience. The training village must have been a leftover from the Second World War; it was very basic, cold and dreary, in need of a good lick of paint. The village part of it could have been a town centre anywhere in the country – it certainly felt real to me at the time – while the only obvious difference from any other high street was a tower at the centre of the complex where the training staff had a good view of what was going on. If the trainees were getting something wrong they could inform us straight away, so we could correct it and not have to wait for a debrief at the end.

In my half-awake state, I found myself wanting to remember more about my own experience. It was the closest I was going to get to what Ross would have to go through in a foreign country. Knowing that this was the limit of my understanding came near to driving me mad with frustration.

So there I was, the night before one of my sons flew into a war zone, with the aim of putting himself in danger – which was almost too much for me to contemplate, let alone say out loud – and I was lying in bed, dreaming, for the first time in ages, about being back in the Force Support Unit (the armed response branch of the Essex Police Force) and our training all those years ago in some run-down army camp.

We were there for two or three days, carrying out our exercises in the village itself, and then storming an old house. We trained on live firing ranges which stretched for miles; the metal targets fell backwards with every double tap I fired – two rounds in quick succession. I imagined Ross had enjoyed it too; I have no idea if they made the training tougher for the Paras, with people shooting back at them, that sort of thing. I imagined him strolling confidently down the main street, his gun resting on his crossed arms in front of his chest as he glanced carefully about him.

When I did this training, the boys were both very young. When they were a little older I separated from their mum, and decided then that I had to leave the FSU and get a different position within the force so that I was there for them more often.

For a while I lay without moving in bed, just staring into the dark, thinking back to Ross's childhood. I tried to recall the moment I'd first held him in my arms. He had the same birthday as my late father – 9 March. The image of Ross as a baby wouldn't come to me. The picture blurred into that of my more recently born daughter Aimee, and when I tried to think of a tiny, newborn Ross it somehow shifted into a collage of moments from Ross's childhood – his first days at school, him falling asleep and me carrying him up to bed, the look of terror on his face when I pushed his little bike fast down a grassy bank — but even those pictures wouldn't stay still in my mind's eye. Instead I saw the times that I'd been a referee, taking charge of the football games that he played with his mates. I had tried to be fair as a ref but in endeavouring to do so I'd sometimes go too far the other way, and lean to the opposing team, especially when faced with a difficult decision. When the games were over I'd take Ross aside to tell him what I thought of his performance, how he'd played, how well he'd done, and where he could improve his game.

These moments didn't always go well, and while I lay there in my bed I tried to recall myself standing there alongside him, my hand resting gently on his small shoulder, and some conversation more satisfactory than the usual one in which Ross sulked and I ended up feeling more fed up than when I'd started. But even though I could still feel his flesh and bone under my hand, I couldn't see his face as it was then. Somehow the grown-up Ross, wearing his customary smile, kept surfacing instead.

I thought about the times we'd argued, when he had been stubborn — or was it me? That didn't do it either: I couldn't wipe the smile off his face. I didn't want to, of course, I wanted him smiling and happy, it was just that I also wanted to try and remain clear on everything I could about him, print everything I could on my memory — because I never knew if I'd get another chance to do so.

I'd spent some of the day before with Ross. Earlier, my wife Tanya had joined us for breakfast, a fry-up in Basildon town centre. It was a nice occasion. I have no idea what Ross was going through himself that day; I only know about my own wide range of emotions. I was nervous, anxious, excited and scared as well. I imagine he was feeling the same, but there was a lot that had to remain unsaid. As much as I did not want to think about it or even admit it to myself, I knew in the back of my mind that this might just be the last time I would ever see him. No parent ever wants to think that they might have to bury one of their own children; parents die before their children do, that's simply the deal.

After breakfast Ross went off to see his mum, and some mates, and get a few last things sorted out. He came round as planned in the evening, to give me his dreaded 'death letter', that I would only ever have to open in the event of his death.

At the railway station we stood in silence, looking at each other. I don't suppose there have been many times when I've just stopped whatever I was doing and looked at someone while they looked back at me. Usually there's something else going on, chatter, distractions of all sorts; but not now. I just stared at him and he stared back. I certainly knew how I was feeling and I could see from the emotion and tears in Ross's eyes that he must be feeling the same way. After a few moments I had to break the tension: I bent forward and we clasped in a manly hug. The hug became a squeeze, neither of us wanting to be the first to let go. I kissed the side of his face where I had kissed him the first time I ever held him in my arms, all those years ago, moments after he was born.

I didn't want to cry in front of him but I knew it would happen. Deep down I am just a big softy and I always get emotional at such moments. I blew out a couple of long breaths to try and stop myself from blubbing like a baby, shook him by the hand, and said, 'Ross. I love you very much indeed.' He smiled back and said, 'Dad, I love you too.' He picked up his kitbag, looked at me, crossed the road, then turned and waved one last time before disappearing into the railway station.

I had nothing left in me then. I was empty and felt naked as the day I was born. Every sinew in my body was ordering me to stride after Ross, to stop him from going, to walk alongside him, to stand in harm's way for him: and I couldn't. This was his job, his life now, not mine, and I could do no more than stand and watch him leave. In my bed, in the early hours of the morning, I realized that what I'd gone through had exhausted me. The emotions churning through me had sapped my energy; but even so, here I was, wide awake. My sons were grown up enough now to stand and fight for themselves, and I was no longer there to stand alongside them.

There's nothing wrong with feeling this but all the same there's no manual that told me what to do when confronted by it — the reality, I suppose, of my own ageing as well as the gradual maturing of my two sons. It's hard enough confronting the realities of getting older, of being stouter and slower than I was 30 years before, without the sensation of fear also creeping in when thinking about my boys. I might have expected to be proudly standing by as they made their way through life, steering them away from some of the mistakes that I'd made, watching them get jobs, meet girls, maybe even take steps towards some thing more permanent. That was something I could have seen coming. But this? Being the parent of not one but two sons heading out to war, of boys becoming men in moments and not years — how was I going to deal with this, at the distance now forced on me? The limited experience I'd had so far of the relationship between the family and the armed forces, the Parachute Regiment and the Royal Marines, didn't suggest that either organization would have too much in the way of help or advice to offer me. I'd have to find a way through all of this by myself, leaning when I needed to on those closest to me.

I thought again about the training village. I wondered how Ross had got on when he'd been there. Had he succeeded in his training? Had he done well? I tried once more to see myself there, alongside him: the two of us together, maybe Luke on my other side. I tried to will that image to take some form of reality for me, as though I could be with them in Afghanistan, in spirit. That's the picture that flashed clearly into my head as I lay there. Where they walked I would walk too.

1

Our Background

My dad, David Wynn, was a bus driver in Leeds. When he was offered a similar job and, more importantly, a brand new three-bedroomed house to go with it, we all upped and moved to the new town of Basildon in Essex, where he became a bus driver with the Eastern National Bus Company. I was only six months old at the time, born in 1958, four years after my sister Teresa.

For the first time in their lives my parents had all mod cons including central heating, hot and cold running water, a fully plumbed-in bath and an indoor toilet. They must have felt like they'd landed on their feet.

Ours was a normal household for the time: dad went out to work while Angela, my mum, stayed at home and looked after the kids and kept the house in order. Mum always made sure that my sister and I were ready for school on time and smartly turned out. She saw that our shoes were nicely polished and that my shirts and my sister's blouses were whiter than white.

Dad's dinner was always ready and waiting for him when he got home. In those days it was still rare for mothers to go out to work. A man was meant to provide for his family.

Basildon was one of the many new towns that sprang up all around London after the end of the Second World War to accommodate the overspill from London's ageing slums. When we moved there, building was still going on everywhere, and great swathes of it were still unfinished. It was simply fantastic to know that we were the only people who had ever lived in our house. I felt like bloody royalty.

By the time I was eight, my dad could still only afford an old second-hand car: a bottle-green Morris Minor with an 1100 cc engine. But it really felt good to have a father who owned a car we could all go out in together. In those days very few families could afford one. All of my mates were jealous. There was only one other family in our street with a car at the time. I remember going out in it one Sunday afternoon with my mum, dad and my older sister to visit an aunt. You could see the curtains twitching in all kitchen windows as we drove away.

I had a great childhood: parents who loved and cared for me, plenty of mates, places to play, trees to climb, green areas to play football in. Time seemed to stretch on for ever, in an eternal present, especially during the long summer holidays.

But this world collapsed when my father died suddenly when I was only 12, in December 1970. The morning he died was very cold I remember. I can still see him bending over his Morris Minor, trying to get it started – which I had seen him do so many times before. If for any reason my father couldn't start the car, he had to insert a cranking handle into the engine through a hole in the front grill. He would keep turning until the car started.

The bus garage where he started work each day was only about five minutes' drive from our home, but he was running late for his morning shift and the car took its time to start.

When he arrived at work he suddenly felt unwell as he got out of the car. He went into the main office and told his boss that he really didn't feel too good at all, that he was going to take himself off home sick, and asked if the boss would be kind enough to go and get him his wages.

It was a Thursday, because that was the day my dad got paid. In those days people were paid weekly in cash, which came in a neat, brown envelope.

As his boss left the office to get his wages, my dad fell off the stool he was sitting on, and was dead before he hit the floor.

I still often stop and think of the horror and carnage that could have been caused if he had died at the wheel of his bus, whilst driving it down a busy road with lots of people on board.

Dad died at about eleven in the morning but I wasn't told about it till four o'clock that afternoon. I was coming home from school with a mate of mine who only lived a few doors away from me in the same street. We were laughing and joking, talking about what we were going to get up to after our dinners and homework.

All of a sudden an uncle of mine emerged from the front door of our house and started walking towards us. I remember thinking that it was a bit strange as my uncle wasn't usually at our house at that time of day. Our families socialized with each other but that would normally be over the weekend and in the evenings. My uncle was a bus conductor who often worked on the same bus with dad. In fact, my dad got him his job. His face was pale and expressionless now as he looked at me.

'Say cheerio to your friend, Stephen,' he said in a monotone.

'Hi, Uncle Mark. What are you doing here?' I asked him, starting to feel slightly uneasy but not knowing why.

'Stephen, listen to me carefully,' he said leaning forward and gently taking hold of my arm. 'I am very sorry, and there is no easy way of saying this, but your father has died.'

Everything suddenly went eerily quiet after that. I could see his lips moving but I just couldn't hear anything he was saying to me. He took hold of my hand and walked me back home. He opened the front door and then it all hit me. The house was packed with neighbours, friends and relatives. They were everywhere: in the kitchen, the hallway, the garden and the living room. My mum was sitting in her favourite armchair next to the fireplace. Her eyes were red and swollen and she was holding a white handkerchief to her face like a soldier surrendering after a hard battle. One of our next-door neighbours, Beryl, had an arm round mum's shoulder.

As I moved around the house I could see all these faces looking at me. Some I recognized and some I didn't. Some spoke words of condolence. Some didn't know what to say and simply settled for the smile you give people when you are not sure what to say.

I made my way round the house in a daze, still trying to take in what was going on. I felt like I was in one of those movies where the camera scans from side to side as it makes its way through a crowd of people and they all stare back. Everybody seemed to be drinking a cup of tea or coffee. I didn't know that we had so many cups and mugs in the house. Everyone who was smoking was polite enough to go out into the back garden to do so. Wherever I appeared, the conversation would stop and only start up again once I had moved past. I was patted on the head or stroked on the arm by the men and hugged tightly by the women – some with massive bosoms, others who nearly took my eye out with their lighted cigarette.

Eventually I managed to get upstairs to the safety of my bedroom. I closed the door behind me and burst into tears. The enormity of what was going on, the realization that my dad was dead and wasn't coming back, hit me like a hurricane. I lay on my bed and just cried.

The pain of that loss stayed with me for many years. In the days, weeks and months after his death I kept thinking that it was all a bad dream and that at any moment he might walk back in through the front door and everything would return to normal. These days the pain has long since gone, and all I have are pleasant memories of those precious years spent with my father, but I will never forget him and he is in my thoughts everyday.

My teenage years were a very strange time for me. I would continually hear my mates talking about the different things they did with their dads, such as fishing, playing football or going to the pictures, and the enjoyment this gave them. These were experiences that I unfortunately never had; but years later, when my sons were teenagers, I was able at long last to enjoy such experiences with them, possibly sometimes doing so even more than they wanted – though, bless them, they never complained.

I've described my feelings about my father and his death at some length because this might help explain my close emotional involvement with my boys, my desire to be there for them and with them. Perhaps we always try to compensate in the next generation for the lack we experienced in a previous one. But there are other connections too, which I only discovered later when I tried to find out more about my dad's life – for my father, like my sons, was in the Army.

He served in the British Army as a member of the Royal Army Ordnance Corps where he was a private. In 1999, I received my father's statement of service record from the Ministry of Defence records department, with the following testimonial attached:

A good average soldier. Hardworking and willing. Reliable, trustworthy, obedient and loyal. Punctual and sober in habits. Neat in appearance. Polite in manner. Military conduct exemplary.

I felt very proud to know that my father's senior officers thought of him in this way. Born on 9 March 1926 in Southend-on-Sea in Essex, he was still only 13 at the outbreak of the Second World War in September 1939. In May 1944, four months after his 18th birthday, he enlisted in the General Service Corps which also comprised the Territorial Army. He didn't see active service overseas and therefore thankfully missed the horrors involved in fighting a war.

He did however serve overseas in the Middle East for ten months in 1947, leaving the Army two months after his return. He re-enlisted in the Royal Army Ordinance Corps Supplementary Reserve in 1951, and was finally discharged from the military in 1955.

I have never been able to find out more about my father's time in the Army. My late mother didn't move to England from Ireland until 1953, by which time dad had already finished his military service. According to her, his time in the military was a topic that never came up for discussion.

Exploring still further back in the generations, I found other relatives with a military past. My grandfather on my mother's side was Private Thomas Byrne who served with the Royal Irish Rifles during the horrors of the First World War. He was one of the lucky ones, surviving and living to the ripe old age of 73. Of seven brothers who served during the Great War, he was the only one to survive that conflict.

According to my mum and her sister, the horrors of war were something he never spoke about either to friends or family. This was common for many of those who fought in it. The sights and memories of what they went through were so horrific that the only way to cope must often have been to try to block out what they had experienced. When you had to bring up a family and hold down a job, you simply could not afford to keep thinking about the war. It was over. You had survived, and now you had to get on with your life.

My great-grandfather on my father's side was a colour-sergeant in the 2nd Royal Lancaster Regiment of Foot during the Indian wars of the 1880s. Whilst serving in India he was unfortunate enough to catch malaria, which was far harder to treat then than today. He was sent home to England and pensioned out of the Army, never really recovering from his illness – which eventually killed him.

I give all this background because it sheds a little light, perhaps, on unspoken memories that probably live on unconsciously in my family, and may even have played their part in my sons joining the Army. And also because, while respecting those who could not bring themselves to speak of the horrors they witnessed, I wanted to choose a different way, and have done so in this book. I feel that what is not expressed may ultimately come back to haunt you. I have drawn much inspiration from the book by the late Harry Patch, *The Last Fighting Tommy*. In his case, he never spoke about his war experiences until he turned 100. It was his firm view that the price of warfare is too great:

It wasn't worth it. No war is worth it. No war is worth the loss of a couple of lives let alone thousands. T'isn't worth it ... the First

World War, if you boil it down, what was it? Nothing but a family row. That's what caused it. The Second World War — Hitler wanted to govern Europe, nothing to it. I would have taken the Kaiser, his son, Hitler and the people on his side ... and bloody shot them. Out the way and saved millions of lives. T'isn't worth it.

Unlike Mr Patch I won't be writing a book about a war that I have personally fought in or one in which I have witnessed great horrors. Nor am I going to wait until his great age to have my say! This book is about a war my sons fought in, and about the emotional effect of this on me.

It was only when my first son Luke was born in September 1986 that the pain of my father's death finally stopped and I was at peace with myself once again. It had been a long journey for me, lasting nearly 16 years, and I was glad it was over. Becoming a parent was a welcome challenge from the moment my wife's pregnancies were confirmed, a responsibility I accepted gladly. As a parent there will be good times and bad times to deal with along the way, when the strength and unity of your family will be tested to the full. Nowhere is this more apparent than when your son or daughter is serving in the British military in a war zone in some far-flung corner of the globe.

For my part I also served Queen and country but in a slightly different guise. At the time of writing this book I had been a constable in Essex Police for 27 years.

I spent my entire police service working as a uniformed officer. CID (Criminal Investigation Department) never appealed to me at all — the expectation was that you put the job first no matter what the cost to your family life or marriage. That didn't seem like a good deal to me. Although it improved over the years, when I first joined the police, CID seemed like a bunch of posers who smelled of cigarettes and cheap aftershave and walked around wearing dodgy-looking suits.

Traffic policing was also a non-starter for me as well. I under-stood the benefits of stopping somebody from dying on the roads by addressing their poor driving. I could also understand it was good to ban people who chose to drive while under the influence of drink or drugs from ever driving again, but I still didn't see that it was a job for the police. I saw police work as catching criminals and locking them up, out of harm's way.

I never even considered promotion. It just didn't appeal to me. The higher up the ladder you managed to get the more money you could earn, but you had to balance that against more responsibility and a great deal more grief.

The only area of specialization that ever appealed to me other than normal, day-to-day uniformed duties was that of a firearms officer. In 1989 I transferred to police headquarters in Chelmsford, where I became a member of the elite Force Support Unit (FSU). The FSU was responsible for all firearms operations and incidents that took place within the Essex police area. This also included providing riflemen and SAS-style house intervention teams.

Each firearms team was made up of a raid team and a support team. The raid team consisted of two officers designated R1 and R2. These were the guys who decided the route that a firearms search would actually take. Then there was the S1 who acted as link between the raid team and the support team, and finally the support team itself. I was the S1 on my shift for the final five years of my time in the FSU, a role I very much enjoyed. The unit also included the Underwater Search and Rescue Unit – or the manky divers as they were endearingly called by everyone else. We also dealt with all major public disorder incidents, such as football matches, fox hunts and demonstrations, along with the usual Friday and Saturday stuff, when party revellers consumed too much alcohol and went out looking for a fight.

We carried out surveillance operations by car or foot. This was an aspect of the work I particularly enjoyed. I wasn't one of life's naturally gifted drivers, but I still enjoyed the thrill of the chase –

being behind a top criminal who had absolutely no idea you were on his tail.

When I started my firearms career we used Smith & Wessen model 10 revolvers and shotguns; and by the time I finished we were using what can only be called machine guns. In my ten years of firearms work I went out on hundreds of operations against suspected armed criminals who had carried out robberies, rapes and murders.

It is strange how attitudes change in relation to what is acceptable or not. When I first started my firearms career in 1988 we were not allowed to display any firearms at all. Any handguns had to be concealed under a jacket, and carbines could not be displayed until they were required for use. By the time I had finished as a firearms officer in 1997 we looked more like SAS storm troopers – with more kit on show than an Action Man doll.

The Force Support Unit was viewed as one of the most elite units within Essex Police, involved in all of the highest profile jobs anywhere in the county. We got the best kit, the best weapons, the best vehicles, and were treated nearly like gods by most of our colleagues. I loved every second of it. Who says there is no place in life for elitism? I would recommend it to anybody. So you see that although I never joined the Army, I did get a taste of the camaraderie, excitement and danger that my sons would later experience in much greater measure, and was able to understand something of both the appeal and the appalling risk.

During my time in the FSU, for example, we undertook anti-terrorist work such as the 1996 hijacking of a Sudanese airline by Iraqi military personnel who had been working in the Sudan as military advisers to the Sudanese Government. They were suddenly and unexpectedly recalled by the President of Iraq, Saddam Hussein. When he had done this previously, the returning military personnel were all summarily executed by his regime. On this occasion they were not prepared to risk the same fate, so taking their immediate families with them on the flight, they hatched a plan to take control of the plane and get the crew to fly them to the UK. Once in the UK, the aircraft ended up landing at Stansted in Essex.

I was part of the arrest team and was also lucky enough to be part of the team that boarded the plane to make sure no more terrorists were hiding on board. There was no fear on my part, just a rush of adrenalin. I was simply doing what I had been trained to do. It was good to have the opportunity to put into practice what we had done in training many times before. Thankfully everything went smoothly, with no surprises. The hijackers had done what they were told to do during the negotiations and as a result nobody was hurt in the operation to regain control of the aircraft.

At one stage the hijackers decided they would come off the aircraft last, after the passengers and the crew. But when it dawned on them that if they did that the SAS might decide to storm the plane, they quickly changed their minds. In fact, the SAS was ten miles away at another airport, so we were on our own with this one! The next day there was a photograph of the operation on the front page of *The Observer*. In the picture you could clearly see five figures climbing the steps of the plane wearing black berets and dressed in dark uniforms. The headline read: 'Special Forces prepare to board the aircraft.' It wasn't the SAS at all. It was me and four of my mates! So according to the press I was a member of the SAS for a day. My claim to fame . . .

Well, that will give you some idea of the work I was involved in. Meanwhile domestic life continued, with its ups and downs. My two sons, Luke and Ross, came from my first marriage, and my daughter Aimee from my second marriage. By the time Aimee was born I was old enough to be her grandfather, but am no less devoted for that.

I am still in contact with both my ex-wives – when I bump into them while out shopping in Basildon, where they both still live, or if we need to discuss one of the kids. I have no children with my lovely third wife Tanya. We are both well on our way to retirement. We have four German Shepherd dogs, all nicely mad in their own way.

So having introduced myself to my readers, it's time to move on to the nub of the matter. You now know a little of my background, and therefore perhaps you can understand some of the feelings I went through — both pride and fear — when my sons were sent on active service to Afghanistan.

2

Strung Out at the End of a Phone: Part One

I didn't actually start out to write a book. Writing was simply a coping mechanism to help me deal with what my sons were going through in Afghanistan. It helped me to deal emotionally with not being able to help them physically. The pages just kept flowing from my fingertips – a cathartic cleansing of feelings.

Many thousands of parents up and down the country have already experienced what I went through, and thousands more will follow in our footsteps during the years to come. I hope that in some small way our story, what we went through and how we dealt with it, can give the general public a sense of what it means to have loved ones in a war zone. Both of my sons thankfully survived their wars and came back to me physically in one piece. For that I thank God. Not all of their colleagues were so fortunate.

I tried to prepare myself for their eventual deployment mainly by talking to a couple of friends and colleagues with sons who served in Afghanistan. I wanted to know how they felt about their sons being in such situations and how it had affected them emotionally; and I asked them if they had any helpful advice. The best they could say was: 'Don't worry. They'll be OK.' At the time it sounded reasonable. It certainly reassured me and made me feel much better. But once the boys' deployment papers arrived, all of that went straight out of the window. The bottom line is that when one of your own is out in Afghanistan it all comes home to you in a totally different way. As a father, I was left feeling almost impotent, because all that I could actually do was sit there and worry. I couldn't pass those same worries on to my sons just in case they, in turn, started to worry about me worrying about them – when they really needed to focus on what they had to do to stay alive.

As their father I had an almost overwhelming feeling that I should have been there standing shoulder to shoulder with them, protecting them, looking after them, and in effect fighting their war for them – but that was totally unrealistic. I couldn't do that, I knew that and so did they. They didn't expect it of me, but it still didn't prevent my protective instinct as a father coming through.

We all live our lives in our own little comfort zones – for most of the time, that is. This in turn gives us a certain amount of control over our own destiny, which we all need. This new experience, however, simply lifted me out of my comfort zone and dropped me down again in a terrifying place.

Looking back on it now, I don't believe that I coped particularly well with the situation I found myself in, though I am not exactly sure how one is supposed to cope and manage or if in fact any amount of preparation can actually help. I felt anxious and afraid for most of the time that my sons were in Afghanistan, simply because of what might happen to them. This wasn't a game. This was war, and in a war people die. I didn't want either of my sons to become casualties of this war.

Both of them made what I believe were very tough and brave choices, enduring lengthy and arduous basic training courses. Both the regiments they joined were the very best – it could be said the elite of the British Army and the Royal Navy – so entry into them did not and could not come cheaply.

The pride that Luke and Ross both had in their respective regiments and the berets they wore on their heads was only surpassed by the pride that I had for both of them and what they had achieved up to that point in their lives – a pride in knowing my sons had stepped up to the plate and passed their tests with flying colours.

In reading this book you will hear about their bravery and achievements both as soldiers and as ordinary human beings. You will also hear a lot about my feelings and the emotional roller-coaster of a journey that I went through while following their progress. For each of them it was six months of their lives, and for me an entire year; but for the three of us it was an experience we will remember for the rest of our days, strengthening the bond between us.

My pride in my sons, as I have suggested, was matched by the stress their exposure to grave risk and danger placed on all of us. Ultimately I have to question, as they have done, whether they were serving a useful purpose in Afghanistan, and whether the cost in human life and psychological trauma is worth the supposed military objective.

But I'll begin with my own, personal responses – including the toll this difficult time took on my own health. Though this might seem like a selfish place to start, I hope it will bring home the kind of feelings parents of serving soldiers go through, and give you a sense of the hidden price of military involvement, far beyond actual injuries on the battlefield.

Back in November 2005 I had two mini-strokes within about six weeks of each other. Since that time I have been on daily medication and periodically had follow-up checks on my thyroid, heart, cholesterol and blood just to ensure that everything is still working OK. In June 2008, while my son Ross was serving in Afghanistan, I went to see my heart specialist, Dr John Stephens. Dr Stephens is what I call an excellent, old-fashioned doctor. He proposed a 24-hour mobile ECG strapped to my body to record my heart rate.

About two weeks later I received a letter in the post from him (which was usual after such procedures). It read as follows:

Stephen, having now had the time to look at your recent ECG results and analyse them, I must be honest and say that I am slightly concerned about your daytime heart-rate. It is running at a much higher rate than I would expect or want it to be at. In the circumstances I would suggest that we double your daily intake of beta-blockers. In closing, I would ask you to consider if there have been any recent and significant changes in your lifestyle that would account for these noticeable changes in your heart rate. I would also like you to come back and see me again in about a month's time so that we can re-run the test.

As a result of receiving this letter I sent an email to Dr David Bullpit, one of the Force Medical Officers (FMOs) for Essex Police, and explained what Dr Stephens had said to me in his letter. Dr Bullpit emailed me back:

Stephen, thank you for your email. I would in the first instance concur with Dr Stephens's observation and ask if there have there been any significant recent changes in your lifestyle.

My reply:

Dr Bullpit, the only thing that I can think of that could possibly be a change in my lifestyle is that my younger son, Ross, who is in the military, is currently in Afghanistan. He is serving with 2 Para, and as you know, over the last few weeks not only have they been involved in some really heavy fighting, but they have also lost five of their numbers. My son has been involved in some of those incidents.

Dr Bullpit replied:

Stephen, I can certainly understand how this could make matters stressful for you, and I would most definitely put this down as both a significant and relevant change in your lifestyle; but try to look on the bright side: in a few months' time your son's tour will be over and he will be rotated out of the firing line and once again be safely back home with you and the rest of his family.

My reply to this was:

Yes, that's true Doctor, but then my elder son Luke, who is serving in the Royal Marines will be rotated in and begin his six-month tour of Afghanistan, so it will start up for me all over again.

Dr Bullpit responded:

> Ah, yes, I see what you mean Stephen. Make sure that you keep on taking your medication and I will see you again in two months' time. Please let me know if there are any significant changes in your health.

I laughed . . . But of course, there was nothing else he could say or do.

But now I want to share with readers a diary of some of my experiences during this time – the ups and downs I went through as I hoped against hope that all would be well with my sons. I often felt helpless and powerless. The only way I could keep in contact was by phone, so much of this chapter is a record of fragmentary phone conversations, with all the frustration this involved. The strange thing about these conversations is that I had to live in two quite different realities at once: I was at home in my familiar surroundings, but at least half of my mind and heart kept being tugged away to a war zone in a far-off country.

A week after I had been for my ECG, I was indoors with my wife Tanya. We had just finished watching football and *Big Brother* on TV. Then the ten o'clock news came on, with headlines that three soldiers had died in Afghanistan. I sat bolt upright and started paying very close attention.

The newsreader went on to say that three members of 2 Para had been killed in a suicide bomb attack in Afghanistan. I jumped up off the sofa and sat closer to the TV. I felt the sudden need to get as close to it as possible. It was as if sitting right up by the screen would somehow bring me closer to Ross. My throat and mouth went dry as dust, and my heart was pounding.

Once I heard the words '2 Para' everything else paled into insignificance. An enormous feeling of dread descended on me. My first thought was, 'Jesus Christ. Please don't let it be my son.' I could see the newsreader's lips moving but I couldn't hear what she was saying. My mind went blank and so I missed the vital words, 'and all next of kin have now been informed'. Then I started to panic. Why hadn't they named the guys who had died yet? Was it because they hadn't managed to get hold of the next of kin? We had been out this afternoon and I had left my phone in the car. My heart started beating even faster. My mouth now so dry I couldn't speak.

I rushed out to the car to get my phone and check for any missed calls or texts. Nothing. Thank God for that. 'OK, now calm down and just start thinking logically,' I told myself out loud.

Tanya started talking to me but with everything going on in my head I couldn't hear what she was saying to me – that all next of kin had been informed. She put a hand on my shoulder to try to comfort me, but by now I was in a world of darkness of my own.

I shouted at one of the dogs out of sheer frustration, but none of them had done anything. I just needed to let my frustration out on something or somebody, and the dogs were the easiest option.

I decided that the best thing was to phone the guardhouse at Colchester garrison. Although the poor guy who answered the phone meant well, he simply couldn't tell me anything at all – which in turn didn't help me but simply left me feeling even more frustrated than I was before. I know that he had probably been on the phone constantly since the news of the guys' deaths had broken, fielding the same questions from concerned families all over the country. I wanted some answers and I was not getting any, which in turn left me feeling even more annoyed and wound up than I had been before. After a few minutes of not getting anywhere, I thanked the guy and put the phone down.

I turned on my laptop to look at the news on the internet, specifically the BBC News website. I immediately saw the words that I wanted to see. 'All next of kin have been informed.' What a huge sense of relief. I nearly burst into tears.

I suddenly felt so much better. It was just like taking a heavy rucksack off your back. But no sooner had I half-collapsed in a heap at the relief of knowing Ross was safe than a massive feeling of guilt hit me at the thought that there were three other families out there somewhere going through the dire emotions I had fortunately escaped.

That evening, surprisingly, I got a really good night's sleep. I woke up at about 6.30 the following morning and switched my mobile on straight away. There were no missed calls or text messages waiting for me. I got up, dressed, and rushed to the petrol station just round the corner, but there was no mention of the incident at all in any of the morning's newspapers. I took solace in the old adage that no news is good news.

I got into work at about 7.30 but my head just wasn't straight and I couldn't concentrate at all. I couldn't keep still. I was fidgeting like a drug addict coming down off his last fix. Although I was physically at work, mentally I was miles away. I flicked through my emails and printed a few things off. I listened to the messages on my answerphone and made a few notes so that I would know who to phone back later. I signed on in my duty book and switched the kettle on, by now really wanting a cup of tea.

At about nine that morning I popped down to the custody area to speak with one of the sergeants who had a son, Marc, who was in the Royal Anglican Regiment at the time and had already served one tour of Afghanistan at the end of 2007. His regiment saw some of the fiercest fighting that the British Army had been involved in since it was first deployed in Afghanistan.

I ran a few things past her about my concerns and worries for Ross. She told me what it was like for her when her son was out in Afghanistan. It was good to talk with somebody who actually knew at first hand what I was going through. She smiled. I thanked her, meeting over.

I went back to my office and, as I climbed the stairs, my mobile bleeped. I put my glasses on and took it out of its cover, and saw that I had missed a call from Afghanistan. I was furious with myself about this, and wound up.

Then I remembered that phones and radios don't actually work in the custody area, which I had completely forgotten. What a time to choose to go there! I just wanted to shout at somebody. I was like an elastic band pulled so tight I was close to snapping.

Then my phone rang. It was Ross. I was ecstatic – really pleased to hear his voice at last.

'Hi, mate. How are you?' I said, tears welling up in my eyes (but as I was on the landing outside my office, nobody could see my momentary show of emotion).

'Yeah, not too bad thanks, dad,' Ross replied in a tired and slightly depressed voice. 'I don't know if you have heard back home but we had a little bit of an incident out here . . .'

I cut across him before he could finish his sentence. 'Yeah, it was on the news last night and there has been a little bit about it in the papers this morning: there have now been a hundred fatalities since the British Army's Operation Herrick deployment in Afghanistan.' I wanted Ross to know that people back home were aware what he and his mates were all going through, and truly appreciated all their efforts. 'Anyway how are you, are you OK? You haven't been hurt or wounded at all?'

'I'm fine, thanks dad. I'm OK.'

'Did you know any of the guys? Were any of them your mates?' I asked, hoping he would say no. I reckoned that it must be bad enough for him at the moment knowing that some of his colleagues had just been killed, but I also knew that it would be a hell of a lot worse for him if they were actually some of his close mates from his time in Catterick.

'They were guys I worked with, but no, I didn't really know them. None of them were my close mates or anything like that,' he said in a very slow, monotonous voice.

My questions became more direct.

'So were you on the same patrol then?' I hoped that once again he was going to say no.

'Yeah, I was,' he said almost matter-of-factly. My heart missed a beat but I took a couple of deep breaths before responding. I didn't want Ross to think that I was stressing out at all.

'Blimey, mate, that must have been a bit scary for you,' I said in as calm a voice as I could manage.

'Yeah, it was. I was about 30 to 50 metres away when the bomb went off,' Ross said. I suddenly felt physically sick and felt like crying. The very thought that my baby boy was only 30 to 50 metres away from serious injury or worse, death, was hard for me to fully comprehend.

'God certainly was looking down on you yesterday. Make sure you keep your lucky rabbit's foot tucked tightly in your underpants mate,' I said humorously, knowing full well that he didn't actually have such a thing.

'I can't say too much over the phone dad. You know how it is.' I was glad he said that because I knew that if we kept on talking about it I was going to get quite emotional and I didn't want Ross to hear that. This was about him and how he was, not about me.

'Anyway dad, I'm going to have to go now as we have to do a few things here kit-wise and I don't want to use up all of my credit in one go.'

'No problem, mate, that's fine. Anyway, you take care and look after yourself and phone again when you can. Thanks for the call, it was great to hear your voice. I feel a lot better now. Love you loads.'

'Yeah, love you too. OK, gotta go. See you later.' The line went dead. I felt so much better after hearing his voice. It was just the tonic I needed. I could feel the stress draining out of my body. I really did feel so emotional about the whole thing and was finding it very hard not to cry.

About a week later, around 9.30 in the morning, I got another phone call from Ross. I was in the office and was really pleased to hear from him again.

'All right, dad! Belated happy Father's Day for yesterday.'

'Thanks very much, mate. Where's my card and present then, you tight git? It's not as if you have been busy recently,' I said jokingly.

He laughed.

'What have you been up to then?' I asked, hoping for a mundane response.

'I've not been back long from a four-hour patrol, which was a bit tasty.' Ross replied.

'Oh, right,' I said almost nonchalantly, thinking to myself that it couldn't really have been that bad.

'What happened then, mate?' I asked.

'Well, we were out on patrol with some lads from SFSG (Special Forces Support Group) when it all kicked off. It was a really heavy contact.'

'Please tell me you weren't injured . . .' My heart started beating fast and a sense of dread filled me.

'No, we weren't, but they certainly were.'

'Thank fuck for that.'

'This RPG (Rocket Propelled Grenade) whizzed past my head and only missed me by a few feet,' Ross said, sounding almost excited as he relived the moment.

'That was a close call. Your guardian angels were certainly doing their job. How many of the enemy did you guys take out then?'

'Quite a few, most of them were slotted by the SFSG, and I think I got one as well,' he said, sounding slightly uncertain and uncomfortable about how he should feel.

'What, you killed one of them?' I was struggling to take in what Ross had just told me.

'Yeah, I think so. I heard someone shout out, "Contact right." I turned round and saw this guy who was about a hundred metres away from me. He was firing at us and then ducked back down into cover. I took aim at where I had last seen him come up; and sure enough he popped up in exactly the same place again, so I just opened up on him. I kept firing and he went down and I didn't see him come back up again. I couldn't say for sure if I hit him or not, but it did the job because he didn't fire back at us again. Maybe he just shat himself with all the incoming fire power that he brought down on himself and got the fuck out of there.'

'Hell, mate, how do you feel about that then?'

'Well, as I said, at the moment I'm buzzing. I don't mean that in a horrible way and I'm not being flash or anything like that; and I suppose later on I will sit down and think about it in a bit more of a mature way, but I haven't been back from the patrol all that long.'

Without any warning the battery on my mobile suddenly died. I couldn't believe it. One minute we were talking away to each other, and the next thing I knew my phone bleeped once, made some funny musical noise and cut out. I didn't have the phone charger with me, and was annoyed because I knew that Ross would try and phone me back and not be able to get through.

Our conversation had been cut off, leaving me with a lot more questions that I'd wanted to ask. But they would have to wait until Ross phoned me back again another day. That might be tomorrow, the next day or next week. So frustrating. But there was nothing I could actually do about it, so there was really no point in worrying. At times like this I found it helped me a great deal if I simply took a pragmatic approach to the situation. Would it change anything if I worried about it? No, it wouldn't. So I tried hard not to.

I went back to my office, sat down, leant back in my chair, rested my hands behind my head and stared blankly up at the ceiling. I still had to try and take in what Ross had told me. After all, I had just heard that he was only a couple of feet away from having his head blown off by an RPG; and then he went on to explain in the very next breath how he had probably killed one of the enemy — how he had possibly taken another human being's life.

I was glad he was alive and uninjured — of course I was. And I was also glad that he had acted so swiftly and done what he had to do when he needed to. But it was still a monumental feeling to know that my son, my little boy, had probably killed someone.

He was alive and his enemy was quite possibly dead. For me that was good. Not so good, though, for the mother and father or the wife of the guy he had possibly killed. But five sets of British parents had lost their sons in the previous week and they were now living through their own personal pain, so I reasoned to myself that Ross was simply doing what he had to do to stay alive and save me from experiencing the feelings of such a sad and painful loss.

For the rest of the day my head was all over the place. I couldn't concentrate or focus on anything at all. In the end I had to take an hour off work and go home early. I wasn't dealing with Ross being in Afghanistan particularly well at all.

While Ross was in Afghanistan I kept my phone on all the time. If I knew that he was phoning, I would stop doing what I was doing, stop talking to whoever I was talking to, or leave the meeting I was in and take the call.

Next time he called he sounded exhausted: 'Today is the nearest I have come so far to thinking I was actually going to die,' Ross said almost nonchalantly.

'What happened?' I tried to sound calm.

'We were out on an arduous, hot, nine-hour patrol. We got about three hours into it when we came across this village. We got about a hundred metres into it when all of a sudden all the villagers did a star-burst back into their homes. As soon as they got back into their homes, all hell broke loose. It seemed like we were taking incoming fire from all directions. It was fucking manic, dad.'

My heart was pounding like the rotor blades on a helicopter.

'I heard about five or six rounds whizz past and then crack as they zoomed past my head one after the other. I just kept thinking that one of them was going to hit me. We all started making for the nearest tree-line to get into cover as quick as we could.'

'Was everyone on your team OK at the end of it or did you sustain any casualties?' I asked, keeping my fingers crossed.

'The bloke in front of me copped one in the leg.'

'Nothing too serious, I hope.'

'I wouldn't exactly say that. He got shot just above his boot line and his leg looked like it was hanging off.'

'Well, your lucky rabbit's foot is certainly working overtime for you Ross.' He laughed at my childish attempt at humour. It was good to hear him laugh. 'Did you manage to locate any of the enemy at all?' For some reason I was trying to avoid the word 'kill'.

'Yeah, we got about five or six of them and the rest of them vanished before we could kill them as well.'

'How did you get the wounded guy out of there?'

'Helicopter. They bring in a Chinook for the actual casualty evacuation, and they also bring in an Apache attack helicopter to shoot anything or anybody who tries to stop us getting the casualty out of there and back to the safety of Camp Bastion.'

'And what about the rest of you guys, how did you get out of there? On the Chinook?' I asked, thinking this was the most logical way for them to get out of there as safely and as quickly as they could. Ross just laughed and said, 'You're joking. We just have to wait for everything to calm down, dust ourselves off and then evac ourselves out of there by route-marching back to the FOB (Forward Operating Base).'

At least, I told myself, he had got back safely, if exhausted, from the patrol.

'I've only got two more days here then it's back to Bastion for a week to relax and unwind and learn how to feel like a human being again, before coming home for two weeks' R & R (rest and recuperation). You don't know how badly I want that.'

'Well, mate it will certainly be bloody good to see you.'

'We can go and do breakfast if you like when you pick me up.'

'Yeah, that will be good. I look forward to it, mate.'

The next time something major happened, Ross was back in the UK, and so the incident – in which three soldiers sustained life-threatening injuries – affected me much less, however guilty I feel about saying it. One of those injured had only just returned to Afghanistan after going back to the UK to attend the funerals of two of his colleagues who had recently been killed in Afghanistan.

Back in Afghanistan again after his short respite, Ross phoned to wish me a happy 50th birthday.

It was really nice to hear from him, especially knowing the effort he was making to phone me, taking time out from his hectic schedule.

Over the next few days, Ross phoned me on about seven separate occasions but for different reasons I missed every call. I was not happy about this at all. In the back of my mind was the thought that every call I missed could end up being the last chance we might ever get to talk. This is why I used to get so annoyed with myself and wound up if I missed one of his calls.

Later that July I was in the office working when a radio announcement said that a member of 2 Para had been killed and two others had been injured in an incident in Afghanistan. Even though once again it said that all next of kin had been informed I still went into my usual blind panic. I phoned Ross's mum at her place of work in London to see if she had heard anything but I only got through to her answerphone.

About an hour later Ross phoned, thank goodness.

'Hi mate, how's you? The incident's been all over the news here,' I said, hugely relieved at hearing his voice.

'How did you hear so quickly, we have only just got back to camp?'

I was now very confused, as it was obvious to me that neither of us knew what the other was talking about.

'I'm talking about one of your guys who copped it and the other two who were injured. That obviously wasn't on your patrol then.'

'Yeah, that was another platoon, not ours. We heard about it but it was some guys from another company and platoon. I was talking about what happened on our patrol,' Ross said, sounding tired.

'So what happened to you then?'

'We were out on patrol when we started taking incoming fire and mortars. One of our guys got blown up by a mortar that landed near him.'

'Fucking hell, mate, is he OK? Alive, I mean.'

'Yeah, he's alive, just about. His whole body was pierced by shrapnel. One bit punctured a main artery in his arm and there was blood pissing out of him everywhere. We had to get him out of there and back to our camp on a stretcher. We were about a mile from our FOB, and me and three other guys were told to stretcher the wounded guy back to the base. By the time we got him back I was absolutely done-in. The terrain was a combination of open ground with no cover and irrigated fields heavy with thick, clinging mud.'

'There you go, I told you there'd be a good reason for having to do the stretcher run when you were at depot,' I said, trying to bring a bit of humour back into the conversation. 'Was anybody else from your platoon injured then?'

'Yeah, our Captain got hit in the knee by some shrapnel but it wasn't too serious and he managed to make it back to base with the help of a couple of the guys. He'll end up with a nice scar to big himself up about when he gets back home,' Ross said more cheerfully.

Strangely, as I was typing up this phone call a couple of days later, the BBC News was showing an item on this same incident. A captain from the Paras was giving an interview and talking about his injury, and I could clearly see four soldiers carrying a guy on a stretcher in the background. One of them must have been Ross, going on what he had told me.

'Every time that we go out on patrol,' he went on, 'we have to go through the green zone which is a couple of hundred yards away from the front of our base.'

'What actually is the green zone? I've heard it mentioned quite a few times now on the news and in the newspapers.'

'It's just that, an area of trees and fields or grass. Hence it is called the green zone,' he said laughing. 'But the trouble for us is that's where the bastards attack us from because they know this is where we always leave our base and start our patrols. On this occasion they just seemed to be waiting for us. The main reason we went out on patrol so early was to get as far into them as possible without them noticing us so that we could then attack them at first light. But we didn't make it more than a couple of miles from our base before they attacked us.'

'So what are you up to now?' I asked.

'Well, as I said, we have only just recently got back to our base after the end of the patrol so I want to go and have a wash and a bit of a clean-up and then try and get my head down, and get some well-deserved sleep.'

'Yeah, I must say you do sound very tired, mate.'

'Tired, I'm absolutely finished. Last night I went to bed at about 9 p.m. as we had to be up for our patrol at two this morning, and I only managed 20 minutes' sleep, because some idiot nicked my mossy [mosquito] net and I have been bitten all over by sand-flies and mossies.'

Then to my annoyance the battery on my phone died again. Ross managed to phone me back later that day and we got to finish our conversation before he had to go and get ready for another night patrol.

I'll fast forward through several more phone calls to the end of July. I was settling into my normal Friday morning workload, updating the custody records of youngsters who had been in the night before to get their reprimands and final warnings. It was just a normal Friday morning to start with. That all changed for me at 11.21 a.m. My mobile rang. I looked at it: no number shown, so when I heard Ross's voice on the line I was somewhat surprised.

'Dad, it's Ross.' Usually when Ross phoned it showed the prefix 01473.

'Hi, mate, how's you? It's nice to hear from you. You OK? You sound very tired,' I said.

'Dad, listen. I've been injured,' Ross said almost nonchalantly.

'Injured? What do you mean? Have you been shot, blown up or what?' My heart was now pounding away.

'Dad, I can't say too much as the call is being recorded.'

'Yeah, but surely you can tell me a bit more than that. I am shitting myself here and my heart is trying to jump out of my fucking chest.' I couldn't really take in what I was hearing.

'Dad, I'm OK, honestly.'

'OK, then just answer me a few questions here and help me out. Have you lost any of your limbs at all?'

'No, I haven't.'

'Have you been shot at all?'

'No.'

'Have you been caught in an explosion?' I asked, by now quickly running out of other possible options.

'No, dad, I haven't.'

'So what the fuck have you done then?' Ross was sounding very drowsy.

'Dad, I can't tell you too much but something will be coming out in the press soon and I wanted to let you know first before you heard it on the radio or TV. I didn't want you worrying.'

I nearly burst out laughing, because I just couldn't help thinking that he really wasn't telling me anything at all. Here he was prepping me before the incident was reported by the press and I still didn't know what was going on.

'So where are you now then? Can you at least tell me that?' I pleaded.

'I'm back at Camp Bastion now. I was casevaced (casualty evacuated) back here with some other guys earlier today.'

'So are you staying there or are you coming back to the UK?' I asked.

'I don t know yet, but I wouldn't think so. Look dad, I'm going to have to go now. I will phone you back later on when I've got a bit more time. OK, take care now and try not to worry.'

'You take care, keep your head down and stay safe. I love you very much,' I said, just managing to control the tears welling up in my eyes.

'Yeah, love you too, dad.' The line cut off.

I was shell-shocked. I didn't know what to do, so I just sat back in my chair, folded my arms and stared at the wall in front of me. My mind was a blank and I wanted to cry. I couldn't help myself. My body started to shake. The more I tried to stop myself from crying, the more my body shook. It was a massive wave of emotion rolling through me and I couldn't do anything to prevent it.

I couldn't understand why I was feeling so emotional, because I knew that Ross was alive and well. I had just spent the last five minutes speaking to him on the phone. I didn't know why, but I suddenly felt so angry, so full of rage and hate. I wanted to hurt somebody. I didn't care who it was, I needed somebody to punish but I didn't know why. It felt as though the beast living inside us all had just awoken in me.

I phoned the Essex Police press office at HQ in Chelmsford to see if they could help me with any phone contacts for the Parachute Regiment barracks in Colchester, so that I could speak with somebody to find out exactly what had happened and just how badly Ross had been injured.

They were very helpful and gave me the telephone number for the guardhouse at the Paras' barracks in Colchester. I phoned and frustratingly got through to an answering service. That is never good at the best of times, but when you are trying to find out something as important as how badly your son has been injured it becomes unbearable. I started to leave a message about who I was, the details of my son and why I was phoning, when all of a sudden somebody picked up. 'At last!' I thought. I can actually speak to somebody and find out what is going on. The person on the other end took my details and then informed me they would get some-body to phone me back as soon as they could.

I reckoned that if it was something really serious they would have told me then and there. But I could still feel this tidal wave of emotion. I simply couldn't move. I was somehow stuck rigid in my chair, frozen in time like a marble statue. I sucked in large gulps of air, trying to calm down; but still the emotion enveloped me. I felt as though I was fighting for my life, trying to thwart a rain of oncoming blows.

I finally managed to free myself from the prison that had become my chair and pulled myself up from behind my desk, leaving the office to set off down the corridor and find my wife Tanya in her office at the other end of the building and a floor below. There was nobody about so I didn't have to worry about making eye contact with anyone, with the risk of starting to blub like a baby.

I went through the door at the end of the corridor and out onto the landing before turning left, immediately catching the glare of bright sunlight full in the face through the giant window running the length of the building. I went down two flights of stairs to the middle landing. Still there was nobody about. Usually by now I would have bumped into numerous colleagues and engaged in some kind of banter with each of them. At that particular moment, if somebody told me I had just won 20 million pounds in the national lottery I wouldn't have paid any attention.

I turned left through the doors and set off down the corridor on the middle floor. I looked into each of the offices one at a time as I passed them all, but thankfully saw only the backs of the heads of people busy beavering away at their desks.

I got within ten feet of the end of the corridor and I could feel the wave of emotion about to inundate me again. Just managing to contain its overwhelming power, I slipped into one of the offices of a sergeant I knew, Kevin McPoland, who was sitting at his desk minding his own business and getting on with his work.

'Hi, Steve,' he said momentarily looking up from the screen of his laptop. 'Give me a second and I'll be with you.' I felt drained. I just started to cry.

'Steve, whatever is the matter, mate?' Kevin asked, not having a clue what was going on. I couldn't speak. I wanted to tell him what was wrong but the words wouldn't come out. It felt like slowly drowning.

By now I was crying uncontrollably. Kevin got up from his desk, walked behind me and gently closed the door to his office but he didn't know quite what to do with me.

'Steve, sit down. What's up? What's happened?' he asked. Still I had my hands up to my face in an attempt to hide the feeling of embarrassment (stupid I know) that I now felt as a result of crying in front of another man. I breathed in four large gulps of air in an attempt to calm myself and regain my composure. I finally managed to speak.

'It's my son. He's been injured in Afghanistan. He's all right and I've spoken to him on the phone so I know he's OK but he can't tell me exactly what's happened to him or how badly injured he is,' I said, still feeling like a complete idiot at being unable to control my emotions.

'Well that's a good start then, Steve. If you have spoken to him he must be reasonably OK,' Kevin said, sounding very relieved that I was now actually talking to him rather than just standing there crying. By now I had started to calm down a bit and compose myself. My pulse wasn't racing so hard.

'Kev, I'm sorry about all of this. I feel such an idiot. I was trying to get down to Tanya's office and all of a sudden this massive wave of emotion just hit me and yours was the first open office with someone in it,' I said.

'Steve, don't be daft, you have nothing to apologize about at all. I dread to think how I would be feeling if it was my son,' Kevin said, switching off his mobile that had started to ring.

'Do you need anything? Is there anything I can do? If you need to go home just go. Give me a ring if there's anything you need. I'm sure that everything will be OK, Steve.'

'Kev, thanks very much,' I said, blowing out a couple of hefty lungfuls of air.

'I'm going to go over the road and have a coffee and try to get my head straight. Once again, thanks for your time.' Kevin gave me one of those 'don't be a wanker' looks. I opened his office door, and off I went to try to get to Tanya's office. It was only another ten feet to the end of the corridor. I made it, then I went through the doors, turned right, then straight ahead – and there she was. I could see her at her desk at the far end of the office, talking with three of her colleagues.

'T,' I called out. She looked up. 'Can I have a word, please?' I said. She could tell simply by looking at me that something was wrong, and as soon as I made eye contact with her I just burst into tears. She threw her arms round my shoulders and held me close. 'What's up?' she asked. Once again I couldn't speak. I knew what I wanted to say but the words simply wouldn't come. My mouth had dried up.

I felt such a fool. By now the other people in Tanya's office had heard the commotion and were looking at us both. I knew that if I couldn't stop crying and speak, Tanya would think that the worst had happened, that Ross had been killed. Once again I found that the only way to regain my composure was to gulp in large gasps of breath. After the third gulp of air I was able to blurt out: 'It's Ross, he's been injured but I don't know exactly how badly.' Tanya continued to hold me close to her not knowing exactly what to say. The firmness and tenderness of her hug was more than sufficient for the time being.

I gently pulled myself away and stood up to my full height – puffing my chest out like an ageing peacock who still wanted to strut his stuff – to make sure I didn't burst into tears again.

'I know he's not injured that badly because I have spoken to him. He phoned me about 20 minutes ago, but he can't tell me what's actually happened or how badly he's been injured, and nobody else can tell me anything.'

Tanya and I stood in the corridor outside her office for about ten minutes, which gave me enough time to calm down again before I started the journey back upstairs to the safety of my office.

It sounds ridiculous, but it felt as if I had been on a military operation simply to get down to Tanya's office; and now I had to fight my way back up and hope I didn't bump into too many people and risk blubbing again.

I made it back up to my office. I sat down at my desk. I thought that I had better get hold of Luke to let him know before it came out on the news, as I knew he would worry once he heard the words 'members of 2 Para'. I knew Luke was away somewhere in Wales on pre-deployment training in preparation for his own tour of Afghanistan. I tried ringing his mobile but it was switched off.

All of a sudden my mobile rang. I looked at the number that came up. It was a mobile number but not one I recognized. I put the phone to my ear. 'Hello.'

'Hello, is that Mr Wynn?'

'Yes, it is. Who's this?'

'It's the sergeant from 3 Para welfare department at Colchester Barracks, sir.'

'Oh, hi. Thanks for phoning back.'

'First of all Mr Wynn, can I just apologize that you haven't received a phone call from us before this, because you should have done so,' he said.

'That's not a problem. I would imagine at times like this you are rushed off of your feet. Please don't apologize.'

'Can I just ask how you actually found out about this incident, please, sir?'

'Yes, of course. It was my son. He phoned me from Afghanistan about an hour ago, but the frustration is that he couldn't really tell me too much about what had happened and how he was, which in turn has only made things even more frustrating for me.'

'That's a really good example of why we don't like the lads to phone home themselves at times like this. We call it self-informing. As on this occasion, it can cause more harm than good.' The guy sounded happy to be proving his point. 'Once again I must apologize that you were not told about this earlier because you most certainly should have been. The delay was largely caused by the fact that your son has been permanently attached to 2 Para since he has been in Afghanistan although he's a member of 3 Para. That is more about our internal procedures than anything else, but our boss has been on to 2 Para to make sure that such delays will not be repeated in future.'

'Thank you, but it's really not a problem; as I said earlier, I am sure that you must be rushed off of your feet when things like this happen.'

'Your son's platoon were involved in a heavy contact with Taliban forces and during that contact some of our guys were wounded. A helicopter was called in to casevac the wounded guys out of there, and during the loading of the wounded, your son injured his back which resulted in him also having to be casevaced out of there and back to Camp Bastion.' I nearly collapsed with relief.

'Hang on a minute, you are telling me that he has simply put his back out? I'll bloody well kill him myself when he comes back. I have just spent the most horrendous hour of my life worrying about how badly injured he was,' I said in disbelief yet joy at the same time. 'Why couldn't he have just simply told me that when he phoned?' I asked, knowing it was a rhetorical question. 'I thought he had had a limb either blown off or a leg amputated or something. I just didn't know what to think.'

'I absolutely understand, Mr Wynn. Look, if there is anything that I can do for you or if you need anything please do not hesitate to call us. I am sure that your son will make a full recovery and will soon be back home and running round fresh as a daisy.'

I felt utterly relieved. I shut my office door and just screamed out as loud as my lungs would let me. I had yet another cry and then looked at some pictures that I had pinned up on my office wall of Ross and Luke from Ross's passing-out parade back in April; and then I burst out laughing.

I spent the next 40 minutes walking back round the police station. I went and saw Kevin McPoland and Tanya to give them all the improved up-date.

I got back to my office again. What I really couldn't get my head round was why I had been so emotional about the whole thing. After all, I had spoken with Ross on the phone and knew that he was basically OK. So why had I burst out crying, and been so completely devastated and unable to control my emotions?

I have shared these moments with you with no holds barred, to faithfully record what I went through without quite knowing why. Having given it some thought, I can only think that the feelings and emotions were not about what had actually happened to Ross, but more about what *hadn't* happened to him, if that makes sense. Perhaps my emotional outpouring was actually about my relief that Ross was alive, that he had not been killed or badly wounded and that he would soon be coming back home in one piece. That made sense to me. I suddenly felt a hell of a lot better about everything.

Two days later, on a Sunday morning, Ross phoned again: 'Listen, dad, I'm still in hospital at Camp Bastion and I'm coming home.' I didn't know whether to laugh or cry.

'Oi, you bugger, you gave me the worst hour of my life the other day when you told me that you had been injured, then couldn't tell me any more, especially when your welfare people phoned me up and told me that you had only put your back out by helping to put some of your wounded mates on a helicopter.'

'He said what? The lying bastard. I did my back in carrying a dead guy's remains nearly two miles back to our FOB. One of the guys attached to our platoon was a dog handler. He had been out with us a few times on patrol but I didn't really know him that well. The poor guy got taken out by an RPG. It actually hit him square in the chest. A mate of mine and I were tasked with putting the guy in a body bag and carrying him back to our FOB. When I picked him up I felt something go in my back but I was told just to get on with it. When we finally got him back to the FOB, about two miles away, we put the guy's remains down and then I collapsed in a heap on the ground because my back gave way and my hip was slightly dislocated as well. I was then casevaced back to Camp Bastion.'

'So when are you actually coming home?' I asked, purposely changing the topic.

'I really can't believe that they fucking told you that, the bastards.' There was a momentary silence before he calmed down and continued. 'I'm not sure when I'm coming back yet, dad. The doctor and physio came to see me this morning and asked if I wanted to stay or go home. I told them I wanted to stay, but then they said I had to go home, which was proper confusing. I hate this place, dad, I'm not going to lie to you, it's an absolute shit-hole. But I want to stay and do my bit. I want to finish my tour with the blokes I started out with.' His tone of voice suggested this was something he felt obliged to carry on with rather than something he had a strong wish for. Like all of his colleagues he had a job to do in Afghanistan and he wanted to do it to the best of his ability.

'Ross, now don't start getting any stupid macho ideas about letting yourself and your mates down. That's utter nonsense. You have done your bit and more. You have witnessed some horrible things. You have seen people die and get blown to bits. You have had to kill people and have come close to being killed yourself. You have stretchered wounded colleagues off the battlefield over long distances back to the safety of your base. You have carried a dead colleague for nearly two miles so that his family could give him a proper, dignified and Christian burial. So don't you dare start thinking that you haven't done your bit, because you are a bloody hero, mate, and don't forget that either. Be proud of what you have done for yourself, your regiment and your country.' I finished just in time as I could feel myself welling up.

There was a muted silence on the other end of the line, so I guess what I said had struck a chord with Ross as well.

'Dad, I'm going to have to go now. Look, I'll try and ring you again later on or first thing tomorrow.'

'OK, mate, take care and keep your head down and hang on to

your lucky rabbit's foot. Thanks for the call and love you loads. Speak soon.'

'Yeah, love you too, dad.' The line went dead.

I really don't know why I kept on mentioning that lucky rabbit's foot. I think that maybe it was partly a kind of magical thinking. Once I had started saying it I felt I had to keep on mentioning it – I was afraid that if I suddenly stopped, bad luck might quickly follow. It was also my way of saying 'you lucky bastard' every time he survived another patrol, especially when there had been a heavy contact and colleagues of his had died or been wounded. We both laughed about it every time I said it, so it also helped lighten what was often a very heavy, ominous sense of things.

He phoned again the next day. 'Hi, mate, how's you?' I said in a bright and breezy voice.

'Yeah, not too bad, dad,' he replied, sounding nice and relaxed.

'Last night was fun, I had some kind of fever and they couldn't get my temperature down below 40 degrees. They are not sure what it was. They thought that I had malaria at first but they have now ruled that out.'

'Bloody hell, mate, it's all happening to you at the moment,' I said, trying to keep the tone of the conversation as light-hearted as I could.

'I had a fan on me all night long and the nurses had to keep sponging me down with cold water to lower my temperature.'

'Lucky you, I hope for your sake that the nurses were women and not blokes,' I said laughing.

'They were women, but dad it wouldn't have mattered what sex they were, how old they were or what they looked like. I couldn't even raise a smile at the moment let alone a hard-on.' We both laughed.

'So any update on when you are coming home then?'

'Should be Thursday or Friday, but I'll find out nearer the time.'

'Well, if your back is totally done in, you might end up not being able to come back during this tour, simply because you won't be fit enough to do so,' I said, gauging by the mood of the conversation that it was OK to say this.

'Don't get me wrong, dad, I want to do my bit, but you know that as soon as I have done my time I'm off... Look dad, I'm going to have to go as I am being told to get off of the phone. They're putting an embargo on calls back to the UK, which usually means that some poor guy has copped it.'

'OK, mate, thanks for the call anyway. Love you loads and I'll speak with you when you get a chance to phone next.'

'Yeah, love you too, dad. Take care.'

At the end of July I was told that Ross was to be flown back to the UK and taken straight to the British military hospital at Selly Oak, just outside Birmingham, for assessment – to see whether he would stay in hospital, go back to Colchester, or be sent somewhere else. I hoped and prayed this would be the end of his tour, since by the time his back was better there would probably be only about three weeks left for him to serve out there.

I didn't hear any more from Ross for a few days although I did hear quite a few times from 3 Para's welfare office in Colchester, in particular a female staff sergeant known affectionately as Ronnie (not her real name). She was very helpful indeed, unlike others I had spoken to who often seemed more like bureaucrats. She updated me on a regular basis and was genuinely interested in Ross's welfare, what had happened to him and about the best way for him to recover. It was very reassuring and nice to know that there were people in his corner who really did have his best interests at heart.

I was genuinely impressed with the support in place behind the scenes, especially as in real terms Ross's injuries were very minor in comparison to some of his more seriously injured colleagues who would be coming home with him.

Once the plane landed at Brize Norton, Ross and the other wounded and injured guys were all driven up to Selly Oak military hospital for individual medical assessments.

Ross phoned me from Selly Oak to let me know that the hospital had only just begun processing and assessing everybody and that he didn't know how long it was going to be before they actually got round to seeing him. I think he now realized he would be staying there for at least one night. I certainly had.

The next morning when I phoned Ross on his mobile he was not a happy bunny at all, not surprisingly. He still hadn't been seen by medical staff. He also felt that he was being messed about by pen-pushing bureaucrats. Back at Camp Bastion in Afghanistan, a blood test result was possible in about an hour, but for some reason back home in the UK it took all day long to achieve the same outcome. Instead of having their own ward to themselves as promised, the guys were simply put in any ward with a spare bed.

Birmingham has a large ethnic population, not all of whom were necessarily in agreement with the British Government's political stance and military involvement in Afghanistan. Given that Ross and the other guys were all still in their desert military uniforms and not in civvies when they arrived at Selly Oak, they did not feel too secure when they found themselves on a mixed ward of people with a whole range of illnesses and ailments. This certainly wasn't what they had been promised – but with all the financial cutbacks going on at the time in relation to military personnel and equipment it really didn't come as that much of a surprise.

At one stage Ross was even told that he would have to stay in overnight on the Sunday as well. Then, adding insult to injury, he found out that the promised lift back home wasn't possible due to sudden staff shortages, even though the welfare department had plenty of notice of the guys' arrival. Instead he was offered a 2nd class rail warrant to make his own way home.

I managed to get hold of Staff Sergeant 'Ronnie' on the phone and explained to her in a very calm manner what the current situation was with Ross. She was not happy in the least. 'No, I'm not having that. I'm just putting my shoes on and I will go and pick him up myself,' she said, sounding as pissed off as Ross. She was absolutely wonderful. It was really nice to see that 3 Para's welfare team was so helpful and professional.

Although the weather was mild, it was raining quite heavily by the time Ross eventually arrived back home at his mum's house on the Sunday evening. Luke and I went out to meet him as he pulled up in the car park. Ross got out of the front passenger seat and, though a bit slow in his movements, seemed all right in himself. He was smiling and appeared genuinely pleased to see both Luke and me. Ronnie opened the boot of her car and Luke collected all his kit – Bergen, body armour and ballistic helmet – to save Ross from having to carry it. He was ever so slightly bent over, and seemed to be in some discomfort, but he also appeared to be in good spirits.

Ross's mum, Tanya, Luke, Ross's best mate Joe and I were all there waiting to greet him. Cindy, his mum, cracked open a bottle of Bollinger champagne which had been in her fridge since the previous December. Ross seemed slightly bemused by it all. Here he was back in the comfort of his own home in Basildon with his immediate family all around him, yet less than 24 hours earlier he had been lying in a hospital bed at Camp Bastion out in Afghanistan.

We stayed at his mum's for about half an hour then left Ross to relax, settle back into his new reality and have a bit of time to himself. As Luke, Tanya, Joe and I left, Ross and I hugged each other in the hallway. I could feel the emotion welling up in him, and he just wouldn't let go of me.

'You let go first,' I said, trying to introduce a moment of humour and spare him any embarrassment he might be feeling. I was just so glad to have him back home safe and sound. He was alive. He hadn't been shot, he hadn't been blown up and he hadn't lost an arm or a leg.

Sunday was a day of rest and chilling out for Ross before he had to return to his barracks in Colchester on the Monday afternoon to be seen for further assessment by the regiment's medical staff.

Over the next few days I had a couple of really good, long conversations with Ross about how he felt about his time in Afghanistan, how he was emotionally coping and how he saw his immediate future. I did my best not to ask him any direct questions about what he had gone through and what he had experienced during his time out there as I didn't want to cause him undue distress.

Having him back had certainly reduced my own stress levels quite considerably. I could concentrate again at long last – which I hadn't been able to do for the past two months. The whole experience had left me something of a nervous wreck, which was very unusual for me.

A major part of my relief was centred on a talk we had about Ross's reasons for joining the Army in the first place. When Ross was about 16, our relationship got somewhat strained for a while (nothing unusual about that; many dads and their teenage sons have fallen out over the years, mainly because the sons were growing up, starting to push at the boundaries, and assert their own identity).

Thankfully, we managed to work through our problems and get things back on track reasonably quickly and without any long-term harm to our relationship. Now, one evening in late August 2008, while we were out walking the dogs, I asked Ross directly why he had joined the Army. He said he thought that it was what *I* wanted him to do and that he believed it would bring us closer together. The slightly humorous bolt-on to that was his belief that if an 'old-fashioned geek' like Luke could complete the Marines' Commando tests then he could certainly do the same in the Paras, standing on his head. Ross had seen his older brother, Luke, who he had previously always perceived as something of a swat and bookworm, join the Royal Marines and stay the course. His perception was that this had brought Luke and me closer together (which wasn't true at all; we had always had a good, solid relationship).

That Ross was so open in his answer about why he joined up showed me that he had matured a lot over the past year.

That was, thank goodness, the end of Ross's first tour of duty in Afghanistan. So I had a brief respite before my other son, Luke, was deployed there in September – a little summer vacation you might say from all the stress and anxiety. We'll come on to Luke's time in Afghanistan in a while.

The last attachment of 2 Para soldiers finally returned home to the UK at the end of October 2008, having completed their six-month tour of Afghanistan. They were met by about 150 of their relatives amidst emotional scenes at their barracks in Colchester.

Fifteen of their colleagues who were either members of 2 Para or who had been attached to them were missing from their numbers. They paid the ultimate price. As well as the guys who had been killed there were another 80 or so of their number who were injured during the tour and had to be flown back to the UK early. The injuries varied from minor things such as heat exhaustion and broken bones to much more serious injuries, such as loss of limbs. During a three-month period throughout May, June and July 2008, the guys in 2 Para came into contact with the Taliban nearly every single time they went out on patrol.

With mixed emotions, Ross went back to Colchester on 30 October to attend a memorial service for the members of 2 Para who had lost their lives whilst serving in Afghanistan between March and October 2008. About six hundred members of 2 Para, many of whom had poignantly pinned red poppies behind the regimental badges on their berets, were cheered on by thousands of well-wishers as they marched through the garrison town en-route to a memorial service at St Peter's Church. The crowd included old soldiers and local residents alike who had all turned out to pay their respects. The regiment had not seen such sustained fighting since their involvement in the Falklands war back in 1982.

Although Ross was a member of 3 Para, for the entire time he was serving in Afghanistan he was actually attached to 2 Para. For some reason I cannot fathom, Ross was not invited to take part in the memorial service and the march-past. From chatting with Ross over a coffee the following day, I know he found it a pleasant yet cathartic experience. It was a way of remembering and at the same time drawing a line under his experiences. He saw many of the people he had served with in Afghanistan, some of whom were part of the parade and some who were simply faces in the crowd. He didn't have too many conversations but a lot of nodding and knowing smiles as he made eye contact with the other guys. One of the things that pleasantly surprised Ross, who was not in uniform, was when a lieutenant colonel at the ceremony recognized him. He was the doctor who treated him in hospital at Camp Bastion. He asked Ross how he was keeping, which gave him a sense of not being forgotten.

Personally, I was extremely annoyed when Ross wasn't invited to take part in 2 Para's parade. He was injured while serving with them, helping to carry a dead colleague's body back to the FOB at Inkerman. His war was over after only two months, but not because he wanted it to be. That was a decision beyond his control. He went out on patrol every day with his platoon when he was based at Inkerman, working, sleeping and eating with these guys. He fought with them. He was with them when five of their own died. He carried dead and wounded colleagues from the battlefield. He was one of them and he became one of their casualties, yet he wasn't even asked or invited to be part of their parade and their memorial service. It might be that they simply forgot, but it certainly did not sit well with me. In my world that is certainly not how we treat and look after our own.

I would like to stress however that the above views are mine and mine alone and have nothing to do with Ross. Maybe I am just being an over-protective parent ... or maybe not.

I've given you my end of Ross's story, my panic and alarm at the end of a phone. In the next chapter I'll fill in some of the details of Ross's actual experiences in the Army, in Afghanistan, and on his return.

3

Ross's Story

Looking back on things now I would say that Ross and I had a good father-and-son relationship. I certainly have pleasant memories of him growing up. We had a lot of involvement with each other mainly through his love of playing football. He played for a local boys' Sunday side. It started off as Basildon Boys' Club but went on to become Kingswood International. He began playing with them when he was a spindly nine-year-old goalkeeper and stayed with them until he was a robust 16-year-old central midfield player.

He was always one of the first names on the manager's team-sheet week after week – not just because I was chairman of the club, but because he was a very good player! In midfield he was solid and dependable. He usually did the midfield holding role, but he also had the drive and ability to know when to push on and support the attack as well.

The team folded after they finished their under-16 season – around the time that young boys become more interested in girls, alcohol and partying. They had been a reasonably successful team over the years and won a few cup finals and league titles along the way. Ross didn't really have too many interests other than his football although he was a good, all-round sportsman.

He got himself a nice little part-time job working in Basildon market three days a week before and after school and then all day on a Saturday. He was very good with his money. He would buy most of his own clothes – usually all brand-named gear. He certainly was a sharp little dresser. But then he worked hard for his money, so why shouldn't he enjoy spending it as well?

When Ross's mum and I split up I bought a half-share in a two-bed flat over in Laindon, on the west side of Basildon. The local council operated a scheme where they owned 50 per cent of the property and you owned the other half. It was the same with the kids, you might say: I had them half the time, and their mother the other half. It seemed to work quite well, though I think Ross, particularly, was hard hit by the break-up.

When Ross left school he went into the building game. It was hard graft and long days which saw him leaving for work at six in the morning and sometimes not coming home until past seven in the evening. He was always paid by cheque, which meant he had to wait for another five days for the cheque to clear before he could get his hands on the money. On more than one occasion these cheques bounced, making the whole process longer and more tiresome.

After about a year of putting up with it, Ross left and went to work for a printing firm. The work was less demanding. He seemed to enjoy it but was never entirely settled. After 18 months or so, his itchy feet got the better of him and he left to join the Army.

Ross started his military life at Pirbright training camp in Surrey where he went on an initial two-day assessment and selection course in March 2007 to check his suitability. How well you do on this assessment determines which regiment you're selected for. Ross did well enough in all of his tests to qualify for the prestigious Parachute Regiment.

When he came back from his two-day 'holiday', as I humorously chose to call it, he was understandably very pleased with himself. But then came the hard part: the journey he went on to earn the right to wear the coveted maroon beret was seven months of intense and sometimes almost brutal training that he would never forget.

His 28-week basic training course started in September 2007 at the Infantry Training Centre at Catterick in North Yorkshire.

I remember saying to Ross what a nice area Catterick was: so clean and tidy. There was no litter lying about and the area wasn't festooned with graffiti on every park bench, shop front or bus shelter. It seemed refreshing to me to be in an area where people appeared to care for their community. Ross's response was, 'You might think it's a nice place but I hate it. I can't wait to get out of there.' But of course he was talking more about the camp than the town itself.

The basic course was a real test for Ross At the six-week stage there was a weekend where family members could travel up to Catterick to watch trainees being put through their paces. Tanya and I drove up to see the boys demonstrating some of the skills they had learnt so far. Afterwards we were taken to their living accommodation to see the conditions that they lived and slept in. It was spartan to say the least – certainly not a home that I would want to live in, but old-fashioned dorms with twelve beds to each area, in run-down buildings dating back to the 1950s or before.

Tamera Platoon, to which Ross belonged, started out with 57 young men. By the time the family weekend arrived they were already down to 30. The 27 drop-outs were partly due to injuries but also because many simply could not put up with the strict mental discipline required to become a member of the Parachute Regiment.

By week nine Ross was seriously thinking about jacking it all in. He only had a week or so to make up his mind because by week eleven he was either committed to staying in the Army for four years with no opportunity of buying himself out or he would have to walk back into civvy street. I didn't try and persuade Ross either way but we did have a couple of long conversations on the phone about it. I said more or less the following.

'Ross, it's your life, mate, and you have to live it for you and nobody else: not Luke, not me, but yourself. This isn't a competition. Luke is Luke and you are you. I don't love you any less or any more whether you stay in the Army or decide to leave it. You have to do what is right for you, Ross . . . If you jack it in now, what will you come back to? I think you might regret it for the rest of your life. I understand you're finding it hard going, especially with all the bullshit you have to put up with, but try to take it one day at a time. Before you know it, it will be Christmas, then Easter, then April and your pass-out parade. Ross, all that I can say is that you are my son and I love you very much no matter what you decide to do. My love is unconditional and I will support you in whatever decision you make.'

The rest, as they say, is history. Ross made his decision and stuck with it as others around him fell by the wayside. I was really pleased that Ross saw it through. Previously, in his short life, every time he had come up against adversity he had taken the easy option and given up. By sticking with it he proved to himself what he was capable of.

The pass-out parade was a very proud day for all of us. All the guys' families and friends sat patiently in a covered grandstand as our loved ones marched onto the parade-ground to the sound of a military brass band. They carried out a very well-rehearsed drill routine and looked immaculate in their olive-green uniforms, maroon berets and shiny black boots. Then they were inspected by the Commanding Officer (CO) of 1 Para and, after a few words of congratulation and a selection of prizes awarded for achievements during the 28 weeks of basic training, it was all over. A salute by the Colonel and off they marched to their respective battalions as the newest members of the Parachute Regiment, to begin their Army life in earnest.

Ross passed out in April 2008, and was then given a few days off before he went to Brize Norton in Oxfordshire to earn his coveted parachute wings. To obtain his wings he had to complete eight parachute jumps from a combination of seven hundred feet, eight hundred feet and one thousand feet. Four of these were night jumps which made it even scarier – for me that is, not him. I certainly couldn't have done it. I could never understand the point of jumping out of a perfectly sound, serviceable aircraft from whatever height it might be. If my life depended on it and somebody pushed me out unexpectedly, then I might – just – be able to do it.

Ross came home for the weekend after the course and then

returned to his barracks at Colchester the following Monday morning. He was only there for a few days before going off to Folkestone for more training. This is a really large area with many different types of firing ranges and a complete replica town where you can train in realistic, pre-deployment conditions. The training included everything soldiers could expect to be called upon to do whilst on operations in Afghanistan. It even included basic class-room tuition in Pashtu, the main language of Afghanistan.

Because of time constraints and the need to get the guys up to speed and out to Afghanistan as quickly as possible, Ross's pre-ops training only lasted two weeks – nowhere near what they needed to prepare properly for their forthcoming six-month deployment.

The main body of 3 Para had already deployed to Afghanistan in early March 2008, and 2 Para deployed in early April as part of Operation Herrick 8.

Ross was given a week off before departing for Afghanistan in May 2008. Earlier in the book I recorded the emotions on both sides when the time actually came for him to leave.

The last time that Ross had been in a Hercules he was jumping out of it somewhere over Oxfordshire. This time he was landing at Kandahar airfield in Afghanistan.

But from here on I'll hand over to Ross himself as much as pos-sible. He was there, and I wasn't, so he should tell it in his own vivid words:

Even though we were wearing our lightweight desert kit, it was so hot when we got off the plane it felt like I was wearing a sheepskin coat buttoned up to the neck. It had been clammy and sticky throughout the journey even with the air con at full capacity, but as soon as we got off the plane it was like walking into a sauna. The sweat was pouring off me.

I felt really good. Here I was at the start of an adventure in some foreign country with a group of my mates – but that feeling didn't last long, I can tell you.

*Before I even got to Camp Roberts I discovered I had been attached to
5 Platoon, B Company, 2 Para. Just me – none of my mates. Just me on
my little old lonesome. I didn't know a single soul in 2 Para so it will
come as no surprise when I tell you that life suddenly got bloody lonely
for me out here. All of them had already been out there for two months
and here I was, the new boy rolling up. I am slowly starting to get to
know the other guys in my platoon now, but it is hard going as they are
nearly all very experienced guys who are on their second tours of
Afghan, and as I am the new guy they think it's a good laugh to give me a
hard time.*

*They are the owners of the gang and they will decide when they are
going to invite me in to join and be part of their crew. The more patrols
you go out on the more you earn your spurs and start to be properly
accepted by the other guys. I suppose that's just the way things are.*

In June 2008, Ross's section was on patrol in the Upper Sangin
Valley, in Helmand Province, when three of his colleagues were
killed by a suicide bomber who, along with a group of other Afghan
males, had stopped to engage them in conversation:

*We were about 2 km into the patrol. It was a very, very hot day, about 50
degrees. I had all of my kit on, my body armour, another piece of kit on
my back and my SA80 weapon. That's nearly 150 pounds in total, and
the sweat was drenching my uniform. My head was so hot that I had a
thumping headache due to a combination of the extreme heat and the
weight of my ballistic helmet.*

*We crossed a river on foot, scanning ahead as we went, and headed
towards the mud-brick compound about two hundred yards ahead of us
at the far end of the fields.*

*My half of the platoon started making its way along a gravel path
while the other half of our platoon was slightly ahead of us and off to our
left. Our natural meeting point was the crossroads at the far end of the
fields and immediately in front of the compound.*

I could see a few of our guys chatting to half a dozen locals about 40

*yards ahead of us as I carried on walking towards the crossroads,
scanning left and right as I went. A few of our guys were talking to them,
and a couple more were watching their backs and just keeping a general
lookout for any danger. Everything seemed fine at first and there didn't
appear to be any problems. As I got about 30 to 50 yards away from the
compound, all of a sudden and without any warning all the locals
vanished, leaving just one of them behind, who detonated the bomb
strapped to his body. All hell broke loose. I wasn't even sure what had
happened at first.*

*Once the noise of the blast subsided there was dust everywhere. I
couldn't see a bloody thing at first. I was absolutely stunned. After a few
seconds my mate Beaumont walked out of the smoke covered in blood
and I thought he was injured from the attack – but it turned out not to be
his blood.*

*We didn't know to start with whether it was a suicide bomber, an IED
(Improvised Explosive Device) or an RPG. All I knew was that it was a
hell of a big explosion and there was smoke and dust everywhere. I could
hear the voices of our Corporals and Sergeants screaming and shouting
in an attempt to get us into formation, and calling in a 9-liner (a pro-
cedure for getting a casualty out by helicopter) and casevac.*

*Some of our guys were shouting out 'Medic, Medic' over and over
again, but it was obvious our guys could not have survived their injuries.*

Ross went on to describe the injuries all these lads sustained as a
result of the explosion. Out of respect for their families, I am not
going to repeat what he told me.

*We called up over the radio to our Forward Operating Base (FOB) for a
Viking armoured personnel carrier to get to our location as quickly as
possible, and explained the reason why. It was with us in under 15
minutes. The guys were all placed in the back of it and transported back
to our FOB.*

*While we were waiting for the Viking to arrive, everybody was in a
kneeling or crouched position, in case there were any other surprises
awaiting us. The tension was palpable and my heart was racing. At*

times like that you can't help wondering what the hell you are doing there.

Once the guys were safely on the Viking and out of there, the remainder of the section carried out a strategic withdrawal. In layman's terms, we simply got out of there as quickly and as safely as we could and made our way on foot back to our FOB at Inkerman.

The terrible thing about this was that we had stopped the suicide bomber two days earlier at a Vehicle Check Point (VCP). Luckily for us, though, he had taken off his explosive vest and left it in a drainage ditch just before he got to our checkpoint. I was one of the guys who were manning the VCP at the time that he went through. We were told all of this at a de-brief sometime later.

We never did find out why he chose not to set the bomb off that day. Maybe he wanted to ensure that he only took British soldiers with him and not local civilians. If he had detonated his bomb that day I would definitely have died.

Even though I was hot, sweating, thirsty, tired and even a little scared, it is amazing what you can do and what you are capable of once the old adrenalin kicks in. When the order was given, my section of the platoon extricated themselves first whilst what was left of the other half of the patrol stood their ground and covered us to retreat in safety.

Once we reached the small river at the other end of the fields we got into our covering positions to allow the other half of the patrol to get out of there. Once we were all safely back over the other side of the river it was heads down and a quick tab back to our FOB, about two kilometres away.

The candidness and passion with which Ross spoke about such incidents was moving, and painted a much clearer picture of what was actually going on in Afghanistan than the British Government seemed willing to admit in the national press.

On his two weeks' R & R, Ross relaxed and unwound in the UK, and on holiday in Ibiza. When he was about to return to Afghanistan I asked him if he was looking forward to going back – knowing full well he wasn't. He laughed and rubbed his face with both of his hands, and said, 'Dad, I've just had a really great time with my mates for the last four days and now all I've got to look forward to is having to go back to Afghanistan and I don't want to go. I know I have to and I will because I don't want to let my mates or myself down, but I fucking well hate it. It's a shit-hole. The place is shit, the people are shit. My work consists of having to shoot and kill people before they try and shoot and kill me. It's bollocks. The Army's not for me and I can't wait to do my time and get out of it.'

He kept laughing nervously and shaking his head in the knowledge and disbelief that in 48 hours he would have to go back to his very own living hell-hole at Inkerman. The more he thought about it the worse it seemed to get for him.

I asked Ross to come home with me and help me take the dogs out for a walk. I think that he was actually glad I had asked. 'Yeah, OK, might as well. I ain't got anything better to do,' he joked.

On arriving home I switched off the engine, got out of the car and went to open the front door. Ross was nowhere to be seen. I leant down, looked into the car and could see that Ross was still in the front passenger seat. I called out. No response. I walked round to see what was up. He hadn't moved. He still had his seat belt on and he was sitting there crying into his hands.

'Oi, mate, come on, get out.' I leant in, unclipped his seatbelt and gently took hold of his arm to help him out of the car. He swivelled round and plonked his feet out of the car. I helped him to his feet and gave him a big hug as he cried on my shoulder.

'I'm sorry, mate. I wish there was something that I could say and do to make things better for you but I know I can't.' Ross sniffed and wiped his nose. 'Thanks, dad, I know you mean well.' He wiped his eyes, composed himself and we went indoors. This was one of those horrible moments. As a parent you are supposed to be there to protect your kids, look after them, resolve their worries, tell them that everything will be all right and keep them safe from danger –

and here I was unable to do any of these things. I felt absolutely impotent and just wanted to cry myself.

Ross and I went out to walk the dogs, took our time and had a chat. There were blue skies, the slightest of breezes, and peace and tranquillity.

By the time that we got back to the house he seemed much more cheerful. The walk and chat seemed to have done Ross some good. We sat in the dining room, had a cup of tea and carried on our chat. After about an hour or so Ross had calmed down. He said cheerio to Tanya, we got in the car and I drove him back to his mum's.

I knew that he didn't want to go back to Afghanistan. Not because he was a coward – because he wasn't; on the contrary, he was a very, very brave young man who had already proved himself in battle on many occasions. He hadn't wanted to be a soldier from about week four of his basic training. As far back as that he knew that he had made a mistake and that the Army and military life wasn't for him. But he didn't wimp out and take the easy option. He dug into his hidden reserves and stayed the course.

I have already described how Ross's tour of duty ended early when he injured his back carrying a dead colleague from the battlefield. But life was not easy for him on his return. I'd like to share a couple of little anecdotes that reveal something of his mood and the things he was trying to come to terms with.

In November 2008, Ross and I met up when he was off for the weekend. He undid his rucksack and pulled out a dark-blue plastic box, handing it to me.

'Go on, open it.' Ross said smiling.

'What is it?' I asked inquisitively

'You'll see.'

I carefully opened the tin. Inside was a bronze medal on a blue-and-white ribbon. The medal had a clasp on it with the initials ISAF, for International Security Assistance Force.

'Wow. That's nice, mate,' I said, really pleased for him.

'It's a NATO medal and everybody who went to Afghanistan got one.'

'Well done, mate. Congratulations. You deserve it.' I smiled with fatherly pride.

'Yeah, whatever. It doesn't mean fuck all to me,' Ross said matter-of-factly.

'You should be really proud of it, mate. You earned that medal. Wear it with pride.' I said to him.

'We can't wear it, the medal or the ribbon.'

'Why's that? It doesn't make sense. What's the point of being awarded a medal you can't wear?'

'It's because it's a foreign-issued medal; we aren't allowed to wear it.'

'It all seems a bit strange if you ask me. Oh well, put it up on the wall in your room.'

'I brought it home to give it to you. It doesn't mean anything to me and I thought you might like it. You can pretend to your mates that you were out in Afghanistan,' he joked.

'Ross that's fantastic. Thanks very much. That's really nice of you. I will put it in the cabinet with all of your other things; it'll be there for you when you have calmed down. I'll look after it for you.'

In December, Ross and I were having coffee together in Basildon. I noticed he seemed quite edgy and not himself. We had a bit of a chat about what he had been up to, and that's when it all came out. He was suffering very badly from constant questioning from his mates about being in the Army. How long had he been in? Which regiment was he in? Had he been to Afghanistan? Had he killed anybody? What was it like being a soldier?

It was all starting to get on top of him – just soldier, soldier, soldier all the time, whenever anyone spoke to him or asked him what he did for a living. He seemed angry, annoyed and even depressed.

I tried to explain to him that this was quite normal because people found what he did very exciting, especially as most of them led routine or boring lives. I also said that some people might be intimidated by him and in certain cases wouldn't know what to say.

My main concern for him was that he would lose the plot and end up punching someone and seriously injuring them, get himself nicked, lose his job and end up in prison.

We were there for about an hour, chatting away but I don't think I helped much. He left still appearing very uptight and angry. I hoped he would calm down in a day or two and that he would start seeing things through normal eyes again.

In January 2009, we were celebrating my mum's 83rd birthday – a nice occasion for the whole Wynn clan. Perhaps I should have remembered that inviting Ross over for a meal or going out for a meal with him on the day he was due to go back to his barracks was not a good thing to do, as he usually had the right, raging hump.

I had told him that dinner was at 1 o'clock and he arrived in plenty of time. He started off fine and appeared in good spirits.

I can't remember exactly when and how it started going wrong for him, but I remember when we were all at the dining table ready to eat he started coming out with some really silly comments about Luke having always been the favourite son.

Ross had become noticeably moody and argumentative after returning from Afghanistan, which he hadn't been before. He didn't seem to be in a nice place in himself at all, and most definitely did not know how to get himself out of it.

It was obvious to me that Ross had been strongly affected by his war experience, and I had to work out a way to try to be more understanding of his plight – yet not be too lenient if he was out of order and needed telling so. Things gradually improved. He has been back now for over eight months, and appears much calmer. He does not seem so angry as he was when he first returned.

I try to remember he was only 20 when he went off to Aghanistan. He saw friends and colleagues die before his eyes. He had to carry the remains of fallen comrades from the battlefield. He experienced many different emotions in a comparatively short space of time and then was dropped back into society with little in the way of support.

It has often been said that there was no counselling offered to soldiers who fought in the First World War and witnessed appalling things. But I wonder if things have changed sufficiently a century later. The expectation is still that a soldier must simply get on with it and pick up the pieces where they left off before going out to Afghanistan. This is certainly how Ross felt about it. Although there are facilities at Colchester where soldiers from 2 and 3 Para can go for help with any issues they might have, in reality this facility is not best used, as it is located within the barracks. Anybody going along to seek such help would be seen going there by their colleagues, attracting attention and possibly derogatory comments.

I imagine that any demons that visit Ross, and take him back to those dire memories, do so in the dark, early hours of the morning and not on a sunny spring afternoon. I must say I am not sure how I would have coped with all he went through at his age.

They say time is a great healer. I sincerely hope this is true for Ross. He seems well on the road to recovery.

One of the good things that came out of all of this as far as I am concerned is the improved relationship between Ross and Luke. It wasn't that they didn't get on with each other before, but simply that they hadn't had too much in common for years. The military aspect of their lives brought them together again. They spent time social-izing, laughing and joking with each other, going for coffees, and sharing their war experiences, knowing that the other would understand. This was all to the good – but a shame, perhaps, that it took a war in a far-off land to make it happen.

Gradually, things improved between Ross and I too. He became less argumentative, less confrontational, and able to laugh at him-self again.

4

Strung Out at the End of a Phone: Part Two

Back-tracking to late August 2008, my other son Luke was pre-paring for active service, and my respite was about to end. 'Will you be leaving me a death letter?' I asked him.

'No. I don't really see the point. We haven't got any unfinished business to go through with each other. I have said everything that I need or want to say to you. We have never had any problems in our relationship as far as I am aware, so why leave a letter? And say what exactly?'

Fair point! I couldn't really argue with that. In the end, though, he did write me a death letter after all.

Luke returned to his barracks in Bickleigh, Plymouth on Sunday, 31 August, for his final preparation for his deployment in Afghanistan.

The following Friday he came back home for a final few days before flying out to begin his seven-month tour. He spent his long weekend chilling out, visiting friends and family, listening to music, playing computer games and coming out with me to walk the dogs.

It was a nice time for me. On the Saturday morning I made breakfast for us all. Even Ross came over. It was good to have everybody together at such an important time for the family. Bacon, sausage, egg, beans, black pudding and toast – and because the weather was so nice we were able to eat it all out in the garden. It was hard to believe that a few days later Luke would be flying off to fight in a war in some distant land.

One evening Luke and I sat down at the dining room table and went through a few of his personal documents, and discussed what he wanted if the worst-case scenario happened and he should be killed. I thought that I had already had this conversation with him and that everything was sorted. Wrong. He went into great detail about what kind of funeral he wanted, who should be invited to it, what music he wanted playing and what to do with his insurance payout. It wasn't an easy conversation: no father ever expects to bury his own son. I put a brave face on the whole thing but I really didn't enjoy it at all. The next day, Wednesday, Luke was back off to his barracks down in Plymouth.

We hugged each other and said our farewells in the multi-storey car park opposite Basildon police station. I didn't have a good day after that. I had a work meeting out at one of the schools I visit, but I wasn't really concentrating as I started to get quite bad chest pains. These didn't get any better as the day went on, so after lunch I went home, went to bed and crashed out for four hours. I was mentally exhausted.

The day finally arrived that Luke had been waiting for and I had been dreading: Friday, 12 September 2008. If it had been Friday, 13 September I would have been even more worried!

Luke had spent all his months of painful and punishing training down at the commando training centre in Lympstone to prepare for this moment. All of those early mornings, late nights, blisters, bollockings from the training staff, lack of sleep, lack of food, being cold and wet, and never quite getting it right now all seemed worthwhile.

He was waiting in line at Exeter Airport en route to Afghanistan via Cyprus. His green 'lid' perched proudly on his head made a nice contrast to his desert-coloured boots and uniform. With all of the excitement of the previous couple of days he hadn't managed that much in the way of sleep and it was the sheer adrenalin of the moment that was keeping him awake.

Along with his mates he had eaten his breakfast just before two in the morning, before loading up all his kit and slipping quietly out of the barracks at Bickleigh in a convoy of unmarked coaches.

The short journey to Exeter Airport took them less than half an hour.

He phoned me from there:

'How are you feeling then?' I asked. 'This is it, no going back now.'

'Actually, I'm all right. I'm really looking forward to it. I just want to get out there now and get on with what I have to do.' He sounded excited. 'It's quite strange really, here I am queuing up with my mates waiting to get booked in and the queue next to us is for Paris, with lots of couples flying off on romantic weekends.'

We had a good, light-hearted chat. Then he said: 'Look, mate, I'm going to have to sign off soon as it's nearly my turn at the check-in desk. It's funny to think that in about half an hour's time all of the things that I take for granted are going to be a thing of the past for a while. Say Hi to Tanya for me. Don't forget to send me some nice parcels full of lovely treats. Have a nice Christmas and see you in January.'

'OK, mate. Take it easy. Keep safe. Do what you have to do. Stay focused and come back to us in one piece. Enjoy the flight. Take care and I love you loads.' I said, just managing not to burst into tears.

'Yeah, love you too, Winnie,' Luke replied very quickly as if he was embarrassed that one of his mates might hear what he had just said to me and think that he was a bit of a wuss for saying it. (Ever since he was a child Luke has called me Winnie, my childhood nickname.)

'OK, bye.'

'Bye.' And the phone went dead.

The roller-coaster had begun again.

Things were slow for Luke to start with. He found the weather very hot, and nothing much was happening. He got to the point of just wanting to get on with what they had come for. He phoned me in September to say they were about to go out on an operation and he would be driving a large lorry in the convoy.

'You're joking, Luke,' I said, 'I wouldn't trust you with the controls to the TV let alone a great big monster of a lorry.'

'Sod you, big man!' he replied. 'Although, if I am honest I would rather not be driving. Look, Winnie, I'm going to have to shoot off now. I will be out of touch for a few weeks so don't panic if you don't hear from me for a while. Dad, before I go, can you send me out some food parcels, please? Super Noodles, none of those rubbish supermarket own-brand ones. Crisps, Haribo sweets, OXO cubes and some decent blokey magazines.'

'Yeah, no problem, mate! I'll get something sorted out. Anyway, you take care, look after yourself, keep your head down and be safe. I love you loads, mate.' By now I was fighting back the tears.

'Yeah, love you too, mate. OK, time to go. I will phone when I can and try not to worry too much. Take it easy, mate.'

It was one of those strange moments in life when you wanted to say so much to each other, whilst knowing that it didn't actually need to be said. The line cut off. I sat back in my chair, put my hands behind my head and smiled to myself, feeling quite good about the world. Having missed a few of his calls I was really pleased to have had this little chat.

As Luke hadn't told me too much about what he was due to be doing and where that would take him I wasn't really sure when I would hear from him again, but I felt fairly relaxed and calm at the time.

Over the next few weeks, there wasn't anything on the evening TV or any reports in the newspapers about incidents involving the Royal Marines. Not a jot, not one article reporting any casualties.

I knew that Luke would be involved in a different type of soldiering from Ross but the risks and dangers were just as great.

The next call came in mid-October. My mobile rang and I knew straight away that it was Luke.

'Hi, mate, how's it going? Nice to hear from you,' I said, getting up from my desk and walking out into the dining room so as not to interrupt Tanya who was watching something on TV she had especially recorded.

'Yeah, not bad, mate! Not bad at all,' Luke replied, sounding quite relaxed.

'What you been up to then?' I knew there would only be so much he would be able to tell me.

'We've been out on a couple of long patrols which lasted for nearly three weeks in total. Not too much happened on either of the patrols, which was a pisser as some of the other companies have been out there doing some real old-fashioned, commando-style soldiering, getting involved in some really good contacts and getting the rounds down.' The enthusiasm with which he spoke about his experiences so far was very infectious.

'The one real contact we got involved in happened on the first day of the second operation. We were driving along in a convoy. I was driving the sixth vehicle in the convoy, when all of a sudden there was this massive explosion up ahead of me in the convoy. It was all very surreal at first. Initially I could not see anything because of all the smoke and dust. It turned out that the fourth vehicle in our convoy had been blown up by an Improvised Explosive Device (IED).'

'Fucking hell, mate, that must have been a bit scary.'

'No, not at the time. Your training takes over, the adrenalin kicks in and you operate on auto-pilot and just do what comes natural to you,' Luke replied. 'I quickly grabbed my medic's bag, jumped out of the cab of my lorry leaving my gunner to look after it, and sprinted up to where the explosion had happened.'

'Nobody copped it, I hope?' I said, suddenly feeling terribly anxious.

'No, thankfully just a few casualties. Two of them were walking wounded and two others had to be casevaced back to our base. They were flown back home to the UK within 24 hours. Both were in a serious but stable condition and expected to make a full recovery. One of the guys had broken all of the bones in his body as a result of the percussion from the explosion.'

'So what did you do then?'

'I dealt with one of the walking wounded guys who wasn't that badly injured, helped him back to the ambulance and stayed with him until medical staff turned up to look after his wounds and injuries. I then took a rifle from the ambulance as I had left mine back in the cab of my lorry and went back to the scene of the explosion as I could hear that it had all kicked off with our guys coming under small arms fire from the Taliban.

'As I got back to the lorry, my gunner was getting the rounds down on a location centred about two hundred yards away. There was so much noise going on with all of the rounds going off that I didn't realize that we were taking incoming, then my gunner shouted at me to take cover as I was being shot at. I won't repeat what he actually said to me but it worked, as it was only then that I realized that the sounds of cracking and whooshing that I could hear were the closeness of the rounds whizzing past my head. I climbed up into the safety of the cab and started firing back along with everybody else. I emptied a full mag in the general direction everybody else was aiming at, but I don't think I hit anybody. It was real gung-ho stuff. It must have lasted about 20 minutes in total and then they stopped firing and vanished back to where they had come from. We cleared the road of the damaged vehicles that we couldn't take with us and carried on with the convoy.'

'Oh well, that wasn't too bad for your first real piece of action. And look on the bright side at least: you came through it unscathed and are still in one piece.'

'That's true. Oh, and the other thing is that I have now been out here for 28 days so that means I qualify for extra pay and the Afghanistan campaign medal.'

'Well done, mate, you deserve both of them. Make sure that when you get your medal you wear it with pride,' I said, knowing how proud I was about wearing my own medals – which were nothing in comparison to those Luke and Ross had both earned.

'Look, I'm going to have to crack on now. I'll phone you when I can but don't panic or worry if you don't hear from me for a couple of weeks or so, it just means that I am out and about on the ground again.'

'Of course, mate. You just concentrate and focus on what you have to do and just phone and write when you can. I do understand, so don't worry.' Luke laughed at the irony of those last few words.

'Oh, I forgot to say: the parcels and letters arrived. Thanks for that. Much appreciated. I got the letters when I was out in the field and the parcels were here when I arrived back. A real morale booster I can tell you.'

'OK, mate, take care. Look after yourself, and I love you loads.'

'Yeah, same here, mate,' Luke replied.

About a week later I was woken up at about 7.15 by two of the dogs, Jerry-Lee and Alfie, wanting to be let out for a wee. Tanya got up while I stayed in bed coughing and spluttering with a heavy cold. For some reason – and I truly don't know why – an overwhelming feeling of dread washed over me in relation to Luke. I started seeing him very vividly in my head: firstly as a young boy in his bedroom when I was married to his mother, my first wife; then a picture of him lying on his bed reading a book. I also had vivid recollections of him training down at Lympstone, the Royal Marines Commandos Training Centre. In the dream he was doing things I had never actually seen him do. Everything was so vivid and real.

I had a flashback to the discussion I'd had with him at the dinner table about his funeral arrangements, down to and including what music he wanted to be played and who he wanted invited. I could also recall the last time I saw him, and us hugging each other goodbye. I could hear his voice from the last telephone conversation we had only a few days earlier when he phoned to say that he was off on a week-long patrol and would be out of contact for a while.

The whole experience was weird – so much so that I got out of bed just to stop myself from carrying on the daydream or whatever it was. For the first hour or so of my day I really didn't feel too good.

Tanya asked if everything was OK. I assured her that it was, and said it was just the cold – which I thought might be true.

We went to the bank for Tanya to pay some money in. As usual we had to queue up there for what seemed ages. While waiting in the queue I saw the clock on the wall above one of the cashiers. The date was 18 October. Then it struck me why I might be feeling this subliminal dread. On the very same day in 1965 my mum's elder brother, James Sylvester Byrne – a sergeant in the Canadian Army – was travelling in an aircraft between Saigon and Hanoi during the Vietnam war, when it disappeared. Although his body was never found it is presumed that the aircraft was shot down.

Nothing did happen that day, and Luke was fine, but it was still a horrible experience, just one of many that I would go through whilst both Luke and Ross were deployed in Afghanistan. Perhaps it shows how sensitive or even over-sensitive one can become as the parent of lads in a combat zone.

Another week later, Luke phoned at five in the morning.

'Hi, mate. How are you?' I asked, wiping the sleep out of my eyes and yawning.

'Yeah, not bad, thanks. I'm back at base now, chilling out and taking it easy.'

'How did your operation go down?'

'Yeah, not too bad. No contacts or chances to get the rounds down, but we discovered quite a few hidden caches which allowed us to recover IEDs, 107 rockets, RPGs, thousands of rounds of ammunition, and a few hundred small arms as well.'

'Well, that's not too bad. Just think of the lives you guys might have saved by recovering that lot. And most importantly of all, you might have found the one that had your name on it,' I said happily.

'Yeah, I suppose so. The really good bit of news though was that we took a couple of prisoners, who turned out to be high-ranking Taliban. One of them was a top quartermaster, which was a massive coup because without him the rest of them won't know where their weapons are hidden as the Taliban work on a secrecy theory, and on the basis that the fewer people who know, the less chance there is of their caches being discovered. And still better, the other prisoner was on the FBI's top-ten list of wanted terrorists.'

'Brilliant, mate, that really was a result then, wasn't it?'

'Yeah, not too bad was it?' We laughed.

'I understand that you guys have just had a time-management adjustment,' Luke said, sounding more like an officer talking in Swahili. You have to remember that it was twenty to six in the morning and I had been woken up from a deep sleep, so I was a bit slow on the uptake at first.

'What the hell is a time-management adjustment? If you mean have the clocks gone back, then yes they have. In fact I have only had about five hours' kip.'

Luke asked how things were back home and how everybody was keeping. I reminded him that Tanya and I were off on holiday to Tenerife in a couple of weeks' time for ten days and it would be best only to phone in an emergency, as it would cost both me and him a small fortune in phone bills.

In mid-November, on the penultimate day of our holiday, I was indoors at the villa where we were staying, having a cup of tea and reading the newspaper. Tanya was outside by the pool topping up her lovely suntan. I had just finished reading the newspapers when my mobile rang. I could tell by the number coming up on my phone that it was a call from Afghanistan. I was immediately concerned because I had told Luke not to phone unless it was an emergency. I had let his welfare people know that I would be out of the country for a while, and the only way that they could get hold of me if they needed to would be by phone.

The phone rang five times before I answered it. I was not absolutely certain who would be on the other end of the line, so I kept my fingers crossed it was Luke.

'Hi, mate, how are you?' said the voice on the other end of the phone. Luke, thank goodness.

'Yeah, not too bad, thanks. Nice to hear your dulcet tones again. Everything OK? Nothing the matter, I hope?' I said, with my fingers tightly crossed.

'No. I'm fine, thanks. Are you home yet or still out in Tenerife? I wasn't sure when you were due home.' The relief was palpable. My heart had started to race, my mouth and throat had gone dry and my palms were sweating.

'We're still there. We will be back home tomorrow night. It's our last day today.'

'OK, well in that case I will keep it brief.' In fact, there is no way that Luke could ever keep any conversation brief. If you asked him how he was, it would be bedtime before he finished answering.

'I don't know if you have heard on the news yet but two boot-necks (Marines) have been killed out here today. I can't say too much about it, but knowing how you were affected when Ross was out here, I thought I'd phone you just to let you know that thank-fully I'm not one of them.'

I was overwhelmed by the same old feelings of total relief that it wasn't Luke who had been killed, yet at the same time accompanied by a sense of guilt. Some other unfortunate family would be going through hell right now.

'No, mate. There has been nothing on the news or in the press, so far, out here and we get all of the usual British channels. Well, thanks very much for letting me know anyway. It really is appreciated.'

'Yeah, I thought that you might want to hear from me just to put your mind at rest. It's sad and all that, and it must be devastating for the guys' families, but at least it's not me.'

'Did you know either of the guys at all?'

'No, not really. They were members of 42 Commando but they weren't in Lima Company. Anyway, Winnie, I am going to crack on now. I might be out of contact for a few weeks so don't worry at all if you don't hear from me for a while, but I won't know for certain for a couple of days when it's all going to happen again.'

'Did you get the mail and parcels Tanya and I sent you yet?'

'Yeah, I think so. Two parcels have turned up. Thanks for that.'

'Did you get the book of poems I sent?'

Luke laughed. 'Yeah thanks for that: a book of poems about guys dying in war. Very cheerful!'

'Yeah, but I know that you like all of that stuff and it was only £2.50. An absolute bargain.' Luke laughed again.

'Yeah, fair one, mate.'

'OK, mate. You look after yourself. Keep your head down. Be safe and I love you loads. Thanks for the call and phone again when you can.'

'Yeah, love you too. OK, enjoy the rest of your holiday and I'll phone again when I can.'

The two Royal Marines who were killed were blown up by a roadside IED in the Garmsir district of Helmand Province. A third Marine was seriously injured in the blast and flown back to the UK. An Afghan soldier was also killed in the same incident. These deaths took the total UK military deaths in Iraq and Afghanistan to three hundred since 2001.

A week after we got back from holiday I had another call from Luke when I was just about to leave for work.

'Hi, mate, how's you?'

'By all accounts I should be dead now and you should be £75,000 richer.' I felt physically sick. Luckily I hadn't had any breakfast yet. This was one of those horrible moments that I had to force myself to come to terms with. Despite how I was feeling inside I had to sound bubbly and upbeat on the outside. I hated not being able to be honest at such times, but I felt that it was more important that Luke kept his focus on what he was doing rather than spend time worrying about me not coping well with his predicament. I thought that if Luke was worrying about me he would not stay focused enough on his job, and a lack of concentration on his part could ultimately cost him his life.

'Mate, what happened?' I asked, not certain I actually wanted to hear the answer. I could feel my stomach tightening and my mouth going dry.

'We were out on an intelligence-led operation when we came across a compound that we needed to enter, search and clear. One of the guys had spotted a local on an old moped but despite our best efforts to get this guy to stop he wouldn't comply. The word went out to stop him because it was believed that he was a dicker (spotter) for the Taliban.' Luke's phone calls always had a slight time delay. If we cut across each other when the other was speaking, it quite often ended up with an answer being given to a different question.

'Eventually our stripey (Sergeant), me and one of my mates managed to stop the bloke. As our stripey started talking to him there was a loud bang which sounded like a car backfiring. It turned out that this guy wasn't a dicker at all, but a suicide bomber. The loud bang that we had heard was the sound of the detonator exploding but fortunately for us the bomb didn't go off.' I didn't know what to say. I was lost for words.

'We found there were some wires sticking out of the front of the bike and three large lumps of C4 plastic explosive hidden in the front of it.'

'Fucking hell, mate, your guardian angels were certainly working overtime again. Did the guy get shot?' I asked.

'No. He was arrested and taken away and hopefully will spend a long time rotting in prison.'

'How do you feel about it all then?' I asked. I felt terrible hearing Luke tell me about it.

'At the time, I didn't really think that much about it at all. Your training just kicks in, but since we've been back at camp I have had a couple of quiet moments where I sat down on my own and thought fucking hell, that was a lucky one.'

This really wasn't doing my stress levels any good at all. I had only recently got back from my lovely ten-day holiday in Tenerife, where I had managed to completely unwind.

'I wasn't sure whether or not I should tell you about it as I didn't want you to start worrying. I was thinking about just hanging on to it all and then telling you on my return, but then I didn't want to risk you finding out some other way and being annoyed I hadn't told you.'

I was glad that he had told me. I had become surprisingly used to these periodic experiences, although I never did cope with them well. If Luke hadn't had these near misses it just wouldn't have rung true. I had learnt with Ross that it was not possible for a soldier to be part of the primary regiment on tour and yet fail to be involved in continuous contacts with the Taliban.

'Anyway, mate, I am going to have to crack on now as it's time to go and get some scran (food) down my neck. I will phone you again soon, just depends on when we are off out next.'

'OK, mate. Thanks for the call – very much appreciated. No matter how bad an incident is, and this certainly ranks up there amongst what I class as bad, I would rather hear it from you than some other medium. No pun intended, of course.' We both laughed at that one.

'You take care. Look after yourself. Keep your head down and I love you loads.'

'Yeah, love you too. Anyway, that's it for now. Speak soon. Bye.'

It was actually very hard for me to take in what Luke had just told me. However, with that type of luck, the odds on him surviving his tour in one piece were, I hoped, very high indeed.

(In September 2009 Luke's Sergeant, who had been with him and another colleague when this incident unfolded, was awarded the Military Cross (MC) for his part in wrestling the suicide bomber to the ground and saving the lives of untold numbers of his colleagues. A very well-deserved award. Luke for one was certainly pleased for him, mainly because his quick reactions that day undoubtedly saved his life.)

The rest of the day was, not surprisingly, a total daze for me. I was in complete shock. The date – Wednesday 19 November 2008 – will be one that I not only remember for the rest of my life, but will celebrate like a birthday or anniversary each year.

C4 explosive is a common type of military plastic explosive, one of whose major advantages is that it can be moulded into any shape you want. The explosive material in C4 is RDX, an explosive nitroamine, which makes up around 91% of the substance. The other elements are plastic binder and marker chemicals such as dinitrobutane and dimethyl, which help to detect the explosive and identify its source. Unlike most explosives, C4 is incredibly stable. You can throw it about all over the place. It can only be detonated by combined pressure and extreme heat or an electric jolt.

The following day Luke phoned me again, but simply to find out if I was OK after the shock he had given me the previous day. I thought this was a nice thing for him to do, and so considerate of him as well. Here he was in a foreign country, without the normal luxuries and home comforts of everyday life, fighting a war; and he still found time out of his busy schedule to phone me to find out how I was holding up.

A few days later, the following report appeared in the *Daily Mail*:

A heroic Royal Marine saved 130 soldiers from certain death when he rugby tackled a suicide attacker before he could detonate a huge motorcycle bomb. The 40-year-old Marine saw the Afghan insurgent reaching for a yellow detonator button on the bike and leapt into action to drag him away.

He foiled a cunningly planned attack in which the motorcycle had been checked by the same troops just hours earlier when its panniers had been packed with potatoes instead of explosives. The suicide bomb contained 70 kilograms of explosives [...]. He tried to set off the first of the bombs but it failed to go off and the Marine was alerted by the distinctive pop of the detonator. He spotted wires running from the bulging saddlebags to another yellow button on the petrol tank and he hauled the bomber off the bike as he reached to press it. The Marine grappled the insurgent to the ground and his comrades rushed in to help him detain the man. Explosives experts later made safe two huge bombs each weighing 35 kilos or five and a half stone, which were packed into each of the panniers on either side of the red 50cc bike.

The Marine, from Devon, who has asked not to be identified, has now been recommended for a gallantry medal. Senior officers believe he saved the lives of most of the 130 men in the area, near Arghandab River, which is just west of Kandahar, including all of those in L Company of the Bickleigh-based 42 Commando. [...]

A couple of weeks later I had to go to Essex police headquarters in Chelmsford, to the occupational welfare department, to see our Force Medical Officer (FMO) Dr David Bullpit. I had been seeing him for about three years since I had my stroke back in November 2005. I usually saw him two or three times a year for a bit of a chat about how I was keeping and if there were any new problems that had cropped up that he should know about.

This session started off with the same question. This time however, instead of my usual response that I was fine, I told him: 'Actually, I am not doing too well at all if I am honest.' I went on to explain about the emotional experiences I was going through due to my two sons being involved in Afghanistan. I explained in great detail my feelings of anger, rage, anxiety, guilt and euphoria, and the reasons behind those feelings. Dr Bullpit seemed somewhat concerned and surprised by my outpourings.

'That can't always be easy to cope with, I imagine, Stephen.'

'Most of the time it's fine. It just seems to come to a head when there has been an incident involving guys in one of my lads' regiments. The anxiety comes while I'm waiting to hear if 'all next of kin have been informed'. When I find out that they have, I start off feeling relieved which is then very quickly followed by feelings of guilt, because I know that somebody else is about to experience terrible grief. When I have calmed down, I start to feel angry and annoyed, as there is absolutely nothing I can do; and I have this sense that I should be out there protecting them and fighting their war for them.'

Dr Bullpit took a sip of his tea then placed the mug gently back down on his desk and shook his head.

'Stephen, would you consider going to see a guy I know who I think might be able to help you? You don't have to go if you don't want to. You can go away and think about it and then get back in touch with me when you have. His name is Trevor Matthews. He's a Reverend and a military chaplain, and also a psychotherapist. I think he might be able to help you. Go along, see what you think and if you are not happy about it or you don't think that it will work for you then you don't have to go back.'

'I don't have a problem going to see this guy. I'll give it a go and see where it takes me. After all, nothing ventured nothing gained,' I said, much to the amazement of Dr Bullpit, who was expecting me to refuse. I suppose there's a general perception that the police have no time for introspection. But we're all human. I made an appointment with Trevor Matthews.

I had another bad fright ten days before that appointment. I was at Woodlands School in Basildon watching Aimee in her theatre group's Christmas show when I got a text on my mobile phone. It was from a colleague of mine at work. It simply said: 'Hi, just hoping your son's OK?' I texted him back straight away.

'Y?'

'Just heard it was a bad day for losses in Afghan so I was worried.'

My pulse started to race.

'It says 4 Marines killed by boy suicide bomber whilst Gordon Brown there on a visit.'

I stepped out from the hall to phone Ross to see if he had seen or heard anything on the news about this incident. He answered his phone at the first ring.

'Hi, mate, it's only me. I've just had a text from a mate of mine at work who says some Marines have been killed by a suicide bomber, but that's all he knows. Have you heard anything about it?' I asked, starting to go into my usual panic routine.

'I'll have a look on the internet and phone you back, dad.'

Less than five minutes later Ross phoned back and read me an article on the internet. It told me what I wanted to know. Luke wasn't one of the guys who had copped it. They were all members of 45 Commando. Three had been killed by the suicide bomber and another was killed by an IED at another location.

I texted my mate back to let him know the good news. Well, not 'good' at all for those who had been killed and their families of course... He then texted me straight back.

'Good. Sorry to panic you.' In the circumstances I don't know who was more relieved, me or him. I then went through my usual feelings of relief and euphoria, quickly followed by guilt.

The three guys had been killed the previous day by a suicide bomber in the upper Sangin Valley, when a 13-year-old boy pushed a wheelbarrow packed with explosives into their foot patrol. All three men were from X-ray Company, 45 Commando, and were based at Arbroath in Scotland. One died instantly, another died of his wounds within a few minutes of the explosion and the third died later at the main British base at Camp Bastion.

It was uncertain if the child was in fact a suicide bomber or just an unwitting casualty of the war who had been duped by the Taliban to push the wheelbarrow towards the troops so that they could detonate the bomb by remote control.

In another incident the same day, a Marine from Whisky Company 45 Commando was killed when the armoured Jackal patrol vehicle he was travelling in was blown up by an IED. He survived the initial explosion but died while being flown to Camp Bastion. Another soldier died on the same day in an incident in Iraq, where it is believed he committed suicide. It marked the worst loss of life in one day for British forces since 14 men were killed back in September 2006 – when a Nimrod aircraft exploded due to a suspected fuel leak.

Two days before Christmas I went for my psychotherapy appointment. The date meant a lot to me, as it was also the anniversary of the first time Tanya and I went out with each other. I parked round the corner from Trevor Matthews's surgery and knocked on his front door. He invited me in and asked me if I wanted tea or coffee. I asked for tea. I am not sure what he read into that or what it meant in psychological terms – but it was a good cup of tea all the same!

He seemed a very nice man. In a previous life he had been a police officer – a sergeant in fact, who had actually worked at Basildon police station as a custody sergeant. He left the police in 1988 to study for the priesthood.

I was there for about an hour and a half. Most of the time I just talked about my life and what I was having problems with, and what I thought the reasons were for the underlying problems. I described the different emotions I was experiencing. Trevor didn't ask me too many questions; he just let me talk and tell him about my personal woes. The session ended with him saying he would write to David Bullpit and tell him how things had gone. He then gave me another appointment for January 2009.

I felt good about the session, albeit tired by the end. I was amazed at how exhausted I felt. After all, I had only been talking – which to me is more or less the same as breathing. Perhaps it was due to re-experiencing all the emotions as I described them. I was getting things off my chest, but also realizing how much there was on my chest to start with!

For more than the obvious reason, 25 December was a day to remember. I came down at about 8.15, still in my dressing gown. I walked into the living room. Sky News was on and running across the bottom of the screen was a yellow headline about a Royal Marine from 42 Commando having being killed in Afghanistan the previous day, Christmas Eve. Once again I went through anxiety, relief, guilt, anger and rage. The situation was made worse for me because the guy was from Luke's Lima Company.

The guy who had been killed, Lance Corporal Ben Whatley, died as a result of enemy fire during a fierce and prolonged battle in the Nad-e-Ali district near Lashkar Gah in Helmand Province. He was the eleventh Marine to be killed in the past two months. A death at any time was hard to bear, but the date of this one definitely made it worse.

It turned out that Luke was also involved in this incident. This was the first Christmas Luke and I had not been together since he was born.

Near to the end of a young Marine's basic training course, and usually after they have finished the demanding and gruelling 30-miler which sees them awarded their much coveted green beret, the recruits have a set of photographs taken. The lads normally purchase lots of these to give to their proud families to own and cherish, as a constant reminder of their loved one's achievement.

One of these photographs is from the waist up in dress tunic, green beret, SA80 rifle with bayonet fixed under the right arm, the bottom of the bayonet in line with the top button of the tunic, white corded lanyard around the top of the left shoulder and head turned to the left, looking straight into the eye of the camera.

I mention this because each time a Royal Marine is killed in action this is more often than not the picture that appears in the national press. Two days later the *Daily Mail* carried this picture of Ben on its front page. The article went on to explain that Ben, like Luke, was due home in a matter of days for two weeks' R & R. I had the luxury of celebrating Christmas belatedly with my son. Not everyone would be so fortunate.

This was getting very close to home – and therefore that much harder for me to deal with. I was becoming an expert at it though. Between May and December 2008 I had gone through this experience at least 18 times. However psychotherapy might help me, it could do nothing to avert the potential death of my loved ones.

I didn't hear from Luke until a few days later on 29 December, so I spent this time wondering what he was going through.

Ben Whatley's death was all the more poignant for us both because it turned out that he was a mate of Luke's. Luke had been on radio sentry duty at the time, which simply meant that his job was to listen into the radio for any messages that needed passing on or acting upon.

Ben was the Lance Corporal of Luke's section. Only a few minutes before they were attacked, Ben had asked Luke to go and take over at the front gate of the compound with a guy from another section. When the attack started, most of the other guys rushed to get up on the roof of the main building that they were in, including Ben. During the resulting attack Ben was hit by a single bullet, and died soon afterwards.

Luke described Ben as 'a real hoofing bloke, a larger-than-life character who all the other guys looked up to'. Luke found his death hard to take and it made him realize just what the emotional cost was of having a mate killed. I think that it also made the entire experience very real and very personal for Luke. He told me later that when they got back to their base after the incident he went off and had a 'moment' to himself so that he could gather his thoughts and try to put things into perspective.

'We are all a bit down about it at the moment as I am sure you can imagine,' he said when he phoned. 'It's only now that we are back from our operation that we can all actually sit down and think about it, collectively and individually. Without it sounding cold and callous you just don't have the time to think about it when you are out on the ground. You have to stay focused and simply lock any other thoughts away in your head and deal with them when you get back to base. That's just the way it has to be. All the guys understand that.'

'The report in the paper described it as quite a heavy fire-fight that you guys were involved in.'

'Yeah, it was certainly that, all right. He wasn't that far away from me when he got shot. It feels strange when I think about it.'

I decided to change the topic so as to try to take his mind off things. I reasoned to myself that it must have been a difficult enough situation for him to deal with, especially as it was still so raw for him and something that so far he hadn't even had an opportunity to grieve properly about.

'So when are you coming back for your two weeks' R & R then?' I asked, knowing that it was some time in January. We went into a bit of old-fashioned code talk.

'Your birthday, and take off ten days, that's when I land back in the UK, but we actually leave Afghanistan on Nan's birthday,' Luke said, sounding like a spy fresh out of training school.

'OK, got that, understood,' I said, trying my hardest not to actually say, 'See you on 7 January then.'

'I will book a few days' annual leave so that we can spend a couple of days together and have a coffee and a good old chat. Do you want a belated Christmas dinner?'

'A family dinner would be nice, but I'm not too fussed about a Christmas dinner as we are having a big one back at Kandahar for all of the guys.'

There was an obvious question I felt I had to ask him: 'Will you be going up to King's Lynn for your mate's funeral while you're back?'

'Yeah, there will be a few of us going up, although we're not too sure how we will be received by the family. Maybe they won't want us to go because our being there might make it an even more painful experience for them,' Luke said.

'Don't be daft, mate. I'm sure that the family will be only too glad to see as many of you guys as possible for Ben's funeral. The article in the *Daily Mail* spoke of his love for the Marines and went on to say that he was living his dream, doing what he always wanted to do since he was at school, side by side with his friends.'

'That sounds encouraging,' Luke said, sounding almost relieved. 'Look, I'm going to have to push on now, Winnie, because I am using up credit from my mate's card.'

'Well, thanks very much for the call. It's really nice to hear from you again after so long. Glad to see that you are safe and well. If I don't hear from you before, I will see you on the date in question.'

'Yeah, should arrive early in the morning at Exeter. I will jump on a train and see you sometime in the afternoon.'

Three days before Luke was due to arrive back in the UK, there was a knock at the door. I answered the front door tentatively, wondering who it could possibly be at that late hour on a Sunday night.

I opened the door only a few inches to stop the dogs running out of the house and scaring the living daylights out of whoever it was.

It was very dark outside. I could just about make out the face of a man in his mid-twenties peering back at me. I didn't take in the man's face and its features but I could see he was wearing a green beret, a sand-coloured Shamog scarf and a desert army uniform. My heart sank to the pit of my stomach. I feared the worst: the knock at the door I had been dreading for the past four months, telling me of Luke's death in Afghanistan. I was finding all of this very confusing because I knew he was due home in three days' time and had therefore already been taken out of front-line action in preparation for his two weeks' leave. So how could he possibly be dead? All these thoughts raced through my brain. To make matters worse the guy smiled at me. I was fuming. Someone just about to break the news of my son's death was smiling at me.

'Hi, dad,' he said.

'Luke?' I said, almost as a question.

'Of course it is. Who did you think it was?'

'Fucking hell, mate, why didn't you phone me and let me know you were coming home early?' I struggled to hold back the tears that were welling up in my eyes.

'I thought I'd surprise you.'

'Surprise me, you nearly gave me a heart attack. I thought you weren't coming home until Wednesday.'

'Yeah, we weren't, but the opportunity to get an earlier flight came up for some of us and not surprisingly we all took it,' Luke said smiling.

'Come here!' I said, hugging Luke as tightly as I could and kissing him on the side of the cheek before bursting into tears. By now I had given up trying to stop myself from crying and just let it all out, which left a wet patch on the side of Luke's desert Shamog. I stood back from him.

'Let me take a look at you,' I said, looking him up and down, then holding him again. 'It's just like a dream. Tanya, pinch me so that I know I'm not dreaming.'

Luke looked resplendent, dashing and debonair in his desert army uniform, his green beret and his sand-coloured Shamog. Not, thank goodness, just a picture in a newspaper. He really did look the part and I was so proud of him.

We carried on chatting away while I went and put the kettle on. Luke got his digital camera out and showed us the pictures he had taken from his time so far in Afghanistan. It was nice seeing images of Luke at work with his mates.

'Tanya, come here. Stand next to Luke and I will take a picture of you both.' Tanya stood next to him.

'Put your arms round each other,' I said smiling at them both.

'Forget you are step-mother and step-son. Tanya, just try to imagine you've been lucky and pulled a soldier on a night out with the girls.' We all laughed. We swapped round and then Tanya took a picture of me and Luke together. To this day both of those photographs adorn my office wall at work. I have always been one for taking pictures on such occasions as they vividly capture a precious moment in time. And in the current situation with Luke on tour in Afghanistan, you never knew if it might be the last chance you'd get.

Both my sons were back, and I could now breathe a sigh of relief and relax. I could start feeling human again, no longer strung out on the end of a phone, hoping for the best, yet always fearing the worst. For now it could only be other grief-stricken families who would mourn the fatalities in Afghanistan.

But my worries were not yet over, for Luke, of course, was going back after his 'rest and recuperation'.

They say that when a monumental event in life happens you can always remember exactly where you were and what you were doing. When Lady Diana died, the news of her death was reported on early morning news bulletins whilst I was indoors ironing a shirt for work. When the Twin Towers were destroyed on September 11, I was at an infant's school in Basildon, watching the horrors unfold on TV. On Friday, 27 February 2009 I was on my way up to Colchester with a colleague of mine, PC Nick Luff, to attend a day's conference on knife crime and the devastating effects it has on families and friends of the victims. We had just turned onto the A130 from the A127 where the two roads meet between Benfleet and Wickford. Nick was driving the hire car provided for the day, a very sporty little Ford Fiesta Zetec. He had just put his foot down to see what speed she was capable of doing (within national speed limits of course!) when my mobile rang. I looked at the phone's display and the word, 'unavailable' came up, indicating that it was not a friend of mine or somebody I knew in a work capacity. I put the phone to my ear;

'Hello,' I said, wondering who it was going to be. To be honest, I thought it was Tanya phoning me from her office. I didn't hear any reply.

'Hello,' I repeated. Again no reply. A moment or two later I could hear a distant voice at the end of the line but I couldn't make out who it was or what they were saying. 'Hello,' said a voice. 'Can you hear me?'

'Yes, I can,' I replied. 'Who's that?'

'It's Luke.'

'Oh, hi, mate. This is a pleasant surprise. The code that normally comes up when you phone didn't come up this time. How are you mate? Hope everything is OK with you and your mates?' As I mentioned earlier, whenever Luke phoned me from Afghanistan there was a slight delay on the phone. There was quite a lot of skill involved in talking to each other in these circumstances. 'Yeah, that's because I'm calling on a secure line this time.'

'Oh, right. Why's that then?'

'Look, dad, I don't want you to worry, but I've been shot,' he said very casually, as if he was simply telling me he had been out fishing.

'Yeah, of course you have, you twat,' I replied, simply thinking he was mucking about and having a laugh after his latest long-range operation in the field.

'No, dad, I have been shot, really. Dad, seriously, I've been shot,' Luke said for a third time. I now realized maybe he wasn't joking, but it was still surreal as he sounded so coherent.

'Fucking hell, mate, what happened?' I said with great alarm, noticing that Nick had now turned to look at me, which was slightly disconcerting as by now we were driving fast in the outside lane of the dual carriageway and he had taken his eyes off the road while negotiating a long, sweeping bend.

'We were out on an op. and I got shot in the shoulder.' I realized Luke's speech was probably so calm because he'd been pumped full of morphine, or 'happy juice' as it is known. It was not otherwise possible to have been recently shot and remain so coherent and relaxed, because of the trauma and stress your body is going through.

'Fucking hell' seemed to be the only phrase I could come out with for the time being. I was like a needle stuck in the same groove on the vinyl. I was in shock. I just could not comprehend what I had heard.

'So what's happening now then? Where are you?' I said almost impatiently. I seemed to have a hundred and one questions inside my head, all jostling to get out. 'I can't tell you over the phone where it happened, but I have been casevaced back to Camp Bastion. I've been shot in the shoulder and thankfully it has missed all of the bones, veins and arteries. It went straight through me and came out of my back. I'm in the hospital there now and I'm just about to undergo surgery. They have got to operate on me, open up the

1. *Ross in October 2007, after six weeks of basic training at Catterick during which he had to walk along a 30-foot high set of poles!*

2. *Luke, Ross and I in July 2007, celebrating my birthday at home. Luke was back during a break in his basic course, and Ross hadn't yet joined up.*

3. *Ross and I at home in July 2008, the night he left to return to Afghanistan after being home for two weeks' 'relaxation and recuperation'.*

4. Luke in the rain waiting to be picked up from the Nad e Ali district in central Helmand, at the end of Operation Sond Chara, December 2008.

5. Ross striking a pose at Kandahar airfield, April 2008.

6. *Ross looking out from a guard tower at Kandahar airfield, April 2008. His blood type, written on his left shoulder, is clearly visible (routine for all our guys).*

7. *Luke listening to his ipod during a break in Operation Sond Chara, Nad e Ali, December 2008.*

8. *Luke, a few minutes after he had been shot, waiting to be air-lifted back to Camp Bastion.*

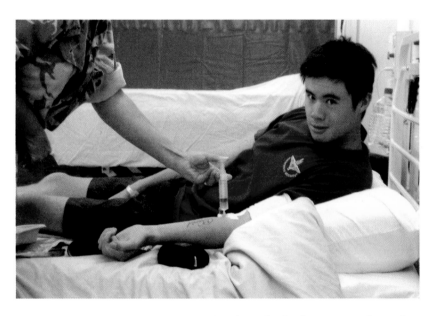

9. *Ross recovering at Camp Bastion in Helmand after being injured in July 2008. He dislocated his hip and damaged the ligaments on the left side of his spine.*

10. At Luke's Passing Out Parade, January 2008, Lympstone.

11. At Ross's Passing Out Parade, March 2008, Catterick Barracks.

12. *Luke being air-lifted back to Camp Bastion after being shot on 27 February 2009 whilst on operations near the town of Khan Nashin.*

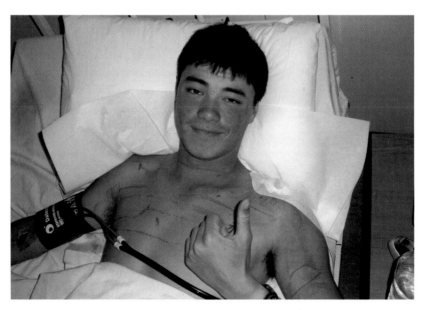

13. *Luke waking up at Camp Bastion, having had his first operation to clean his wounds.*

14. Luke 'relaxing in South Helmand in a lush green zone on the banks of the River Helmand (an area known as the 'Fish Hook', due to the prominent bend in the river), February 2009.

wound and clean it all out. Look, dad, I'm going to have to go now, but I'll phone you back later on this evening when I've come out of surgery. Don't worry, I'll be fine.'

I didn't really know what to say. I was speechless, helpless. One of my sons was in a hospital bed thousands of miles away with a gunshot wound and I couldn't do anything to help. That was the deal when you had a son in the armed forces on active service. All you could do was be there for them in a spiritual sense, and pick up the phone when they called.

'OK, mate. I will speak to you later. Thanks for the call. Love you loads,' I said, struggling to hold back the tears that were trying their very best to burst out and turn me into a blubbering wreck.

'That was my son who's in Afghanistan. He's been shot. I can't believe it,' I said, pushing myself back against the headrest of my seat, breathing a large gulp of air and then blowing it back out again twice as quickly.

'Shot?' Nick said, shocked himself.

I could hear and feel my heart beating away like an old brass drum. I made the phone calls I needed to make — to Ross, Tanya and Luke's mum, giving them the bad news but reassuring them at the same time. I was strangely calm myself, but at the same time deeply troubled.

We arrived at the conference just after nine o'clock. I spotted the Inspector in charge of territorial policing

'Boss, can I just have a quick word with you, please?'

'Yes, of course you can, Steve,' he replied looking at his watch.

'I might have to slope off during the course of the morning today. On the way here this morning I received a call telling me my elder son had been shot in Afghanistan.' The Inspector looked at me with a sudden urgency on his face.

'Steve, I didn't even know that you had a son serving in Afghanistan,' he said, sounding shocked. 'Steve, you do what you need to do. That goes without saying. I totally understand.'

'Cheers, boss. Much appreciated.'

I made small talk with a couple of people I recognized but I wasn't really listening to what they were saying – not out of rudeness, I was simply unable to focus on anything for more than two seconds at a time.

We sat towards the back of the hall. I reasoned that if I received an urgent phone call from or about Luke, or if it simply all got too much for me, I could slide out without making too much fuss and noise. I sat through the first part of the day, up to the morning tea break at 11.20.

I really wasn't paying attention to any of the speakers. I simply could not concentrate. I could see their facial expressions and their mouths moving, but I couldn't hear a single word that they were saying.

Before I knew it the morning tea break arrived. I felt like a junkie coming down off crack cocaine. I was fidgeting, rolling the fingers from one hand round the fingers on the other hand, stamping and twisting my feet, rubbing my forehead, scratching my beard and looking at my mobile phone to see if it was ringing (I had it on silent). I was staring at the portraits on the wall, the hall's interior furnishings and the grain in the wooden flooring.

'Nick, if you are OK with it I am going to go now, but I don't want to spoil your day,' I said, almost apologetically.

'Steve, don't be daft, mate, we can go any time you want,' Nick said.

'OK, let's grab a drink and a biscuit and disappear.'

I phoned Ross en route and explained that we were on our way and we would be at his barracks in about ten minutes. Ross came racing up when we arrived. We drove back to Basildon together. I went and had a hug with Tanya and updated her about what had happened and how the day had gone. I had a few loose ends to tie up workwise, then Ross and I went for a coffee. 'So how are you with all of this then, Ross?' I asked, taking a sip of my drink.

'Not too bad. Looking forward to seeing him home now... He

certainly knows it isn't a game now. I will guarantee you that once he has had time to sit and think about all of this he won't want to go back out there again. It's a shit-hole, dad, and unless you have been there you can never fully understand what I mean.' He was starting to sound slightly agitated. 'I'll tell you now, I ain't never going back there, no matter what the cost is – even if I end up in the glasshouse. Me and Luke have both run up our luck accounts on these tours, and I for one ain't ever gonna try and look fate in the face a second time. I ain't sure that the dice would roll the same way for me the next time.' By now he was talking in gangster rap-style. Perhaps this was his way of dealing with what he felt about Luke getting shot.

Luke phoned me again just after six in the evening.

'Hi, mate, how's you?' said a slightly groggy-sounding voice on the other end of the phone.

'I'm fine, thanks, but more importantly, how are you?'

'Yeah, not too bad in the circumstances. I came round from surgery about half an hour ago. I think I was in there for about three hours whilst they were doing what they had to do.'

'OK, and did everything go OK? According to plan, I mean?' I asked, my fingers crossed tightly.

'Yeah. I think this operation was to clean the wound out. Get all the crap and gunge out of it and to check round inside to make sure that everything was still where it should be.'

'You had many stitches then?'

'None, actually.'

'None, what do you mean none? Surely there must have been lots of them?'

'No, because they haven't actually stitched me up. They have left the wound open so that in a few days' time they can take another look at it to make sure there is no infection and that everything they have already done has taken as it should.'

'OK, right. So what's next then?' I asked.

'They'll monitor me over the weekend and operate again on Monday; and if everything is OK, they will stitch me up then.'

'OK, take it easy. Love you loads and I will speak with you on Monday.'

'Yeah, love you too, bud.' I suddenly felt very calm and relaxed now that Luke had been shot. I suppose that I felt like this because I knew that his war was over and that he was coming home at long last after six gruelling months of combat. Luke phoned back before his next operation and again at about 6.30 in the evening after it, sounding slightly groggy but also in good spirits.

'Hiya. How did it all go then?' I asked.

'Yeah, it was OK. I'm a bit sore at the moment, which is only to be expected I suppose, but they have stitched it all up so I am assuming that it all went OK,' Luke said with slightly slurred speech.

'Well, that's good, mate. So where do we go from here then?' I said.

'I think that I am still here till about Wednesday and then I fly down to KAF (Kandahar Airfield) in readiness to fly home to the UK on Thursday.'

'Do you know what is happening yet when you get back to the UK? Are they sending you up to hospital in Selly Oak, straight back to your barracks or are they thinning you out when you land and letting you come home?' I asked, hoping he would say he was coming home.

'Don't know yet, mate. I think they will let me know either Wednesday or Thursday, but as soon as they do I'll phone and let you know.'

'OK, mate.'

'If they do thin me out when I land back in the UK, could you pick me up from Brize Norton? If not, no problem, mate, I will get a train back.'

'Of course I will. It would be a pleasure. Just let me know what time you're landing.'

'I'm going to slope off now as I'm feeling very tired,' Luke said yawning.

'OK. You take care and I will speak to you later in the week then. Love you loads.'

'Yeah, love you too.' I left to collect Luke from Brize Norton just before lunchtime on the Friday morning, with Ross.

We parked up, confirmed that Luke's flight was still due to arrive on time and grabbed a coffee and a quick bite to eat. There were lots of other families waiting round in the arrivals area for their returning loved ones. The flight had guys returning home because of the injuries they had sustained whilst fighting in Afghanistan, also soldiers coming home for their two weeks' R & R, and others who had completed their six-month tour.

We had been waiting for about 30 minutes when, rather than coming through the arrivals door in front of me, Luke suddenly appeared behind me, having been dropped off at the front of the terminal. I managed to hold back the tears as Luke stood in front of me in his desert uniform, looking slightly dishevelled, tired and in need of a good shower. His left arm was bound tightly to his body in a sling. We hugged each other gingerly, both trying our hardest not to knock his shoulder.

'That was a bit sneaky. Here I am waiting with my eyes glued to the arrivals doors and then you sneak up on me from behind,' I said laughing.

'Well, mate, that's what you get with a properly trained, steely-eyed dealer of death,' Luke said, smiling.

'How are you feeling then? How's the shoulder holding up?'

'Yeah, not too bad, thanks. It's a bit sore and the stitches feel a bit tight, but other than that it's fine.' Luke pulled down his shirt to show me the wound.

'Blimey, mate, I can't work out how the bullet didn't hit your collarbone and shatter it. You are certainly one lucky bugger.'

Ross and I followed Luke out to the front of the terminal where there were lots of other soldiers milling about waiting for transport, and loved ones to come and pick them up. They included six other Royal Marines, who, like Luke, had sustained minor injuries. Most of the guys were waiting for their kitbags before they could begin their onward journeys either back to their barracks, to hospital in

Birmingham or back home with their families, friends and loved ones.

It was becoming obvious that there was some kind of problem with Luke's luggage. Luke and a couple of his mates went to have a chat with the RAF personnel in charge of the luggage.

They reappeared ten minutes later, and not in the best of moods. 'They have gone and lost our effing kit. Can you believe it? They have one job to do and they can't even get that right.' Right now, Luke looked more like a coiled spring than an injured soldier. He and his mates all had to traipse back inside to fill out some forms in relation to their lost kitbags. Finally we set off for home, giving a lift to a colleague of Luke's, a fellow Marine. The mood in the car was quite buoyant – different conversations going on between the four of us at different times about the numerous experiences they had had whilst out in Afghanistan. It was nice for me to see Ross taking an active part in the conversation, which he seemed to be enjoying. It was as if he was back in the thick of things.

'So, Luke, are you still going on this course in November you were telling me about,' I asked, 'or has this put the kibosh on things?'

'Yeah, I certainly hope so. It just depends on whether or not I'm back by then,' he replied matter-of-factly. I wasn't exactly certain what he meant by that.

'Oh, that's good,' I said, excitedly. 'Have you made your mind up about going on holiday to America?' Luke laughed.

'What are you laughing about?'

'Oh, didn't I tell you?' Luke asked in that matter-of-fact way again. 'I've volunteered to go out to Iraq. If I get it, I'm due out there in July.' I had just got used to the idea of having him safely back home in the UK and a more peaceful, less stressful life for me; and then out of the blue he hits me with this low-baller.

'Oh, that's good, mate,' I said, lying as only a father can in these situations. 'How long will you be out there for then?'

'The tour is for between two and three months and I will be

stationed in Basra,' Luke said, as if that was going to make things any better for me, especially as it had become a magnet for every suicide bomber in Iraq over recent months.

'So how did this come about?'

'It was mentioned whilst we were on tour, and I fancied having a go at it, especially as we ain't going to be out there for too much longer and it will most probably be my only chance at getting another medal, so I thought I'd give it a go.'

Later that evening, Luke and I were having a bit of a chinwag about him getting shot and how it had happened and what he thought about it. During the chat he took off his 'Lightning Lima' T-shirt to show me his freshly stitched wounds. I just couldn't make out Luke's wound at all. When you looked at him square on it was hard to understand how the bullet had missed his collarbone. It should have been shattered; but luckily for him when the bullet struck him he was leaning slightly forward. It therefore only skimmed the top of his collarbone, travelled right through his body, missing major arteries and organs, and exited his back just above the shoulder blade.

Other than the two relatively small scars that now adorned either side of his left shoulder, Luke had got off quite lightly. He was taking it in his stride, and luckily it was a comparatively minor wound that would heal up nicely, with no unpleasant, long-term effects. I wasn't sure I could say the same about the state of my soul. And the thought that Luke had volunteered for Iraq was one that went on worrying me below the surface.

5

Luke's Story

No brothers are ever exactly the same, and Luke and Ross had always been like chalk and cheese. They even fought like cat and dog when they were younger. Even though they were brought up exactly the same, with the same standards and morals, they were worlds apart in most respects.

When they were young kids in primary school, they were quite close to each other. Luke was the eldest by only 18 months, so there was only one year between them at school. Once they both reached secondary school they grew so far apart that they had very little if anything in common.

Like Ross, Luke attended the Kingswood Junior School as a youngster, but after passing his eleven-plus with flying colours he attended the prestigious Westcliff High School for Boys near Southend. Whereas Ross excelled in sport, Luke shone academically. He strolled through his secondary education, obtaining an amazing 13 GCSEs – six of them As and another six Bs, before going on to achieve 3 A grades at A level.

Luke was on his way to Bangor University in Wales to study English and Criminology but then decided to take a gap year before beginning the next stage of his academic life. Having spent the last twelve years of his life studying, I think he just wanted a break from it all for a while.

He decided to get a full-time job so that he could save some money towards his university fees, and went to work in a local bookshop as a sales assistant. Three months into his gap year, out of the blue, Luke decided he would join the Royal Marines and become a Commando. Or, as he put it, a 'lean, mean, fighting machine'.

Luke and I have always had a good, solid relationship. I can't actually remember that we ever clashed with each other – just the odd, mild disagreement which we sorted out amicably.

I never had the same involvement with Luke as I did with Ross when he was young, because Luke wasn't into sport. He was into endlessly reading books. No sooner had he started reading a book than he had finished it – incredible to watch. He also had the ability to remember everything he read with amazing accuracy.

At primary school he had been in a local Cub Scout group. He always knew the answers to the questions the Scout masters would ask, so quite often they would ignore Luke when he put his hand up, just to give the other kids a chance. He only did it for about 18 months or so but he had nearly every badge it was possible to earn. The sleeves of his green Cub-shirt were festooned with merit badges. Luke could tell you what every single one of them was for without pausing for breath. His other main interest was War Hammer, which involved collecting different toy soldier armies and using these in game combats with other kids and their armies. Luke used to spend hours gluing them together and then carefully painting them in a particular colour scheme. He had hundreds of the things. When it came to birthdays and Christmas it was never a problem knowing what to buy him. Sometimes I wondered if he was becoming a bit of an anorak. I certainly had to pinch myself often to remember how young he was. I had more intelligent conversations and discussions with him when he was younger than I managed with many adults. My chief interaction with Luke as he approached his teenage years was an hour and half on a Saturday morning when we popped down to Basildon for a coffee and sandwich. We would drop Ross off for his football training at about 9.30 in the morning and pick him up again at midday. It was really nice for me and Luke to have a good chat. If he had any problems he would let me know, and we would just sit down and talk them through.

We are quite close to each other without actually being close in interests, if that makes sense. He certainly appears to have my sense of humour, is quite laid-back and easy-going about most things, as I am. He always champions the underdog and leaps to the defence of people if he thinks they are being unfairly treated. But I certainly cannot claim he got his brains from me. I was an average GCSE student, while Luke was an A-star A-level student.

Ross and Luke were also miles apart when it came to their reasons for embarking on life in the military.

Luke initially wanted to be a fighter pilot when he was at secondary school. He was actually set on it in a big way. He had already considered joining the RAF so that he could train to become a fighter pilot and be funded to study for a degree at the same time. What eventually put him off was discovering that after finishing his full-time education he would have to study and train for a further six years to realize his dream.

Although he had decided that a life in the Royal Marines was what he wanted, he appeared to be dragging his heels somewhat when it came to actually getting on and doing it. At one stage he told me that he thought that the Marines only had two intakes a year. I remember telling him not to think or assume, but simply go away and find out what the truth of the matter was.

Luke had a tough time of it during his basic training, but it also showed his steely determination – a trait not always apparent in his personality up to then.

He originally went on a four-day Potential Royal Marine Course (PRMC) in October 2006. Though he tried his best, he actually failed the course, but the instructors obviously saw something in him that they liked because they offered him the chance to try again and gave him a three-week fitness course first. He went straight from that course to another PRMC, which he passed in December 2006. He began his basic course in January 2007 as a member of 938 Troop.

Although the basic Royal Marines Commando course is only 32 weeks, it would be more than another year before Luke left the Commando Training Centre (CTC) at Lympstone as a fully-fledged Royal Marines Commando. The Royal Marines course is universally acknowledged to be one of the toughest military training courses anywhere in the world.

Luke stayed with 938 Troop for the first 16 weeks or so of his basic course before injuring his left knee. Due to ligament damage he then left them and joined Hunter Troop, which is where Royal Marines recruits are sent if injured. Hunter Troop has a world-class physiotherapy team, also used by Premier League football teams and Olympic athletes.

Luke was concerned that once there he would simply be forgotten. The record for being there was over two years, set by some poor guy who broke his leg during initial training. By the time the guy passed out as a Royal Marines Commando he had already served enough time to quit the corps. Luke, though, was only in Hunter Troop for about two months before he managed to get himself back into mainstream training with 943 Troop. He hadn't been with his new buddies for more than five minutes when the injury flared up again. He managed to keep himself out of Hunter Troop this time round, wangled himself some sick leave bolted onto a period of leave, which gave him and his knee some time to recover and a nice long period of rest. He got back on track and returned to 943 Troop in November 2007, just in time to complete his Commando tests, which culminated in the 30-mile yomp across the wilds of Dartmoor.

The evening of the day he completed the 30-miler and earned himself his coveted green beret he phoned me to let me know he had done it. He was in a certain amount of pain and discomfort, he said, but what kept him going was the thought of failing it and then having to phone me up and tell me!

Luke's passing-out parade was in January 2008 at the Commando Training Centre at Lympstone. Ross managed to get a couple of days' leave from his training in Catterick to come down. It wasn't the best of days for a pass-out parade as it rained so heavily the Royal Marines had to revert to plan B and move the ceremony inside. Even then it was still very cold. Luckily we were all wrapped up in overcoats or jackets.

Luke looked resplendent in his Royal Marines dress uniform, with a white peaked cap. It was a very proud day for me. I now had a son who was a qualified Royal Marines Commando. The Royal Marines started life in 1664 as part of the Royal Navy when 1,200 soldiers of the Admiral's Regiment were divided into groups of 200 men and spread among King Charles II's fleet of ships — and they still regularly get the mickey taken out of them for this by other regiments in the British Army. During the dark days of the Second World War, there were as many as 78,500 men serving as Royal Marines. The current figure is approximately 6,500 men who serve either in 40, 42 or 45 Commando.

Several months passed after this before Luke was deployed in Afghanistan in the autumn of 2008. This was just as well, as Ross was out there during that time. I can't imagine how I would have coped with two sons being in a war zone at once.

You've already heard about some of the incidents Luke was involved in, which he told me about over the phone. Here's a description in his own words of one of the operations:

The entire (anti-Taliban) operation went on from 27 November until 31 December, but Lima Company was dropped in on the 11 December and we came out on 29 December. I think that we were in the mix for about 18 days in total. The battle for Zarghun Kalay went on for four days solid. At one stage we didn't get any sleep for over 36 hours. By the end of it we were just hanging out. In total we covered about 60 kilometres of terrain.

Until Luke showed me the report of this operation in *The News of the World* I hadn't heard anything about it. Luke seemed amazingly matter-of-fact about it all, and his part in it. It was called *Operation Red Dagger* after the shoulder-patch insignia worn by the 3 Commando Brigade. Around 1,500 soldiers took part, and by the end of it five of them had been killed, four of them Royal Marines, and another 80 of them had been injured. The purpose of the operation was to capture and secure four major insurgent bases at Nad e Ali, Shin Kalay, Zarghun Kalay and Nawa.

Lima Company was involved in fighting at both Nad e Ali and Zarghun Kalay. We were getting ready from 2 December, then finally left Camp Bastion on the night of 11 December and flew by helicopter to the Helicopter Landing Site (HLS) Oslo which is situated in the south-west of the province – known in military terms as 'route Somerset'.

At one time it rained continuously for three days. We set off for Zarghun Kalay at about 1.30 in the morning on 17 December, and soon after we left it started pissing down. We yomped till about 4.30 a.m. and we then went static [stopped] for about two hours.

I'm not too proud to tell you that I nearly went down that night. When we went static, that was horrendous for me. I was soaked through to the bone and to make it worse it was freezing cold and I nearly lost it. The real pisser was that with all of that rain our weapons and magazine pouches started to go rusty, a sort of orange colour, because we could only oil the internal working parts in the middle of all the dust and sand that was always blowing about. They took some cleaning later I can tell you.

Our last operation contact was at a place that we knew as Yellow Four. I don't know what its actual name was, but that's what we called it anyway. It was like a small village. That was where Ben copped it.

As Luke said this, he almost bowed his head in respect. 'There's never a good time to lose a mate and a colleague, but that close to the end of the operation must have made it harder to deal with . . .' I said. Luke didn't say anything but simply nodded his head in agreement.

Yeah, it wasn't nice, especially as Ben was a mate, but at the time you just have to get on with it. Some of us had our quiet moments when we got back to Bastion and our Sergeant told us that nobody would be thought any the worse of if they wanted or needed to shed some tears.

It was amazing for me to sit there and listen to my son tell me these things, as a seasoned professional. It made me feel very proud to know that he was, and had been for some time, a man in his own right. He was and always would be my son, but he was also his own man now. Not a chip off the old block, not a younger version of me. He was an original in his own right, whose own son would some day point proudly at him and say, 'That's my dad!'

You have already heard how Luke got shot on his first tour of duty. A month before, while he was back in the UK, the following little incident occurred. I report it here to show the kind of strange and unsettling encounters soldiers can have when they return to so-called 'ordinary life'. It often isn't an easy adjustment.

Luke went shopping, and to get a haircut. While in town he was, for want of a better word, accosted by three local 'hard cases' who thought it would be fun to tangle with him. Wrong place, wrong time, wrong person. One of the idiots asked Luke 'if he was all right'. Luke replied that he was fine, thanks; and then they starting taking the piss out of him because of his 'posh' accent. Luke said that in normal times he would have just walked away from it all, and ignored the entire thing. But something inside him snapped.

It obviously didn't help matters that Luke had already lost twelve of his colleagues during his first four months in Afghanistan and that the very next day he was going to the funeral of a mate who had been killed on Christmas Eve. Luke rounded on the three guys.

'Do you know where I have been and what I have been doing for the past four months?'

'What?' the one who was using the single brain cell they shared between them replied, whilst the other two just stood there looking gormless.

'I'm a Royal Marine, you twat, and for the last four months I've been fighting in Afghanistan, so do you honestly think that you and your two girly mates here scare, frighten or worry me in the slightest?'

Mainly because this wasn't the response that the three were expecting they didn't quite know what to say.

'Well, it was your choice to go to Afghanistan, nobody asked you to go. What do you want, a fucking medal?'

Not even thinking about backing down or worrying about the potential outcome of taking on these three idiots, Luke kept up the offensive.

'I've had people shoot at me, try to blow me up, try to kill me, and you and your fellow twats here think you can frighten and scare me. You must be even more stupid than I first thought you were. Now take your girlfriends here, and fuck off.'

The red mist started to descend very quickly over Luke. But not wanting to be outdone by Luke's manliness, the ringleader came back at him with one of the feeblest statements of the century.

'I've just come out of prison after being banged up for four years mate, so don't think I'm frightened of you, because I ain't.'

'What, and you think that makes you hard, mate? All that makes you in my eyes is an even bigger twat than I first thought you were. So take your girlfriends here, and do one.'

Once again, Luke walked on, thinking that was the end of the matter, only to find out a couple of minutes later that it wasn't.

The idiot who had already had two miserable attempts at trying to scare and intimidate him just couldn't let it go. He thought he had to keep up the misplaced pretence that he was a hard man. He chased after Luke for a second time, pulling out a motorbike chain from under his jacket.

'Come on then, mate. I ain't afraid of you. What, you think just because you're a soldier that I'm scared or worried? Well, I ain't,' he said, trying to convince himself of his own invincibility. 'Come on then, you and me round the back now,' the guy said, repeatedly swinging the bulky chain round his head.

'First off, I ain't a soldier, I'm a Marine, and do you honestly think that after facing the Taliban with their guns, knives and bombs out in Afghanistan, that I am afraid of some twat like you with a girlie fucking motorbike chain?' Luke then pulled off his sweatshirt and threw it to the ground. 'Come on then. If you really want to try and prove just how much of a poof you actually are, then let's do it. Bring your girlfriends with you to make it a fairer fight. I'm telling you though, the first one of you I get hold of, I am going to hurt. So before we start, just decide amongst yourselves which one of you wants to be hammered. I don't care how much I get hurt, it won't stop me hurting the guy I get hold of.'

Luke by now had totally lost the plot. The situation wasn't helped by the immaturity and total failure of his assailants to know when to back down. This wasn't because of any backbone or heroism they possessed (clearly they didn't), but purely because none of them wanted to lose face in front of each other and passing members of the public.

Luckily for these three idiots, just before it all kicked off a guy whom both Luke and I knew arrived on the scene. Luke used to go to primary school with him and I had nicked him a few times over the years. He had a reputation amongst his peers for extreme violence and had already served two prison sentences for violent offences.

'Oi. Leave him alone and back off,' said this character. 'Not only is he a mate of mine, but you really don't know who you are messing with. You will need more than the three of you to take him out. Now do yourselves a favour and fuck off, before somebody calls the old bill.' At least the three troublemakers had enough savvy to recognize a gift horse when they saw one.

'Just think yourself lucky, mate. He saved your neck. I'm telling you. Next time you might not be so lucky,' the ringleader said, backing off and making out he had won the day but really knowing he hadn't.

Luke picked up his sweatshirt, smiled his acknowledgement to his old schoolmate, ran an imaginary knife across his throat and pointed at the guy with the bike chain. 'Next time, mate, next time you won't be so lucky. If you have actually got a brain, then realize just how lucky you have been here today. Don't bring yourself to my attention again.' There followed some trading of insults, and before the police turned up they had all disappeared into the crowds of shoppers.

I saw Luke at home less than an hour after this incident, and he was still seething. He told me all about it, and when I had finished listening to him I quickly realized this just wasn't like him at all. I also realized just how lucky the other guy was not to have got himself very badly hurt or worse. And I was also alarmed at the thought of what trouble Luke could have landed himself in if this had happened.

Such a contrast: on the one hand an idiot who spends his entire life thinking he is hard, just because he can't string a coherent sentence together, has a skinhead haircut and walks as if he has a broom permanently up his backside; and on the other hand Luke, who may look and even sound like a geek but is a Royal Marines Commando. Yet the fact that Luke even came near to getting mixed up in this scene may say something about the stress and trauma he'd been through, and had not yet fully come to terms with.

6

Two Sons — Two Ceremonies

Medals have always been important to me — a symbol of achievement, of hard-earned merit — and their ritual presentation at award ceremonies seems a helpful way to acknowledge this achievement in a memorable occasion.

My Long Service & Meritorious Conduct medal for 22 years' service in the police was awarded at a very nice ceremony in 2005, followed by a buffet at the Guildhall in Chelmsford. Luke and Ross came along, as did Tanya, which made it even more of a special occasion for me. The Queen's Golden Jubilee medal I was awarded in 2002 was simply left unceremoniously in my tray at work — so no special occasion to mark that one. Nevertheless I was still as proud as punch to receive mine and it is displayed in my living-room cabinet along with other similar mementoes.

So this brief chapter is a small interlude in what may otherwise be quite a harrowing tale. Such ceremonies — even if they're not well organized as you'll see — at least allow us to stand back and take stock, have a breather and try to realize the meaning of what we've been through. This does not mean, of course, that they can undo the horror and trauma that young men witness daily in Afghanistan or other war zones, but they can at least celebrate these men's incredible bravery.

Ross phoned me in November 2008 to invite me to the award of his campaign medal for serving in Afghanistan. 'Guess who's presenting us with our medals then, dad?' he said.

I didn't have a clue. I just hoped it would be someone worthy of the honour.

'Go on then, put me out of my misery. Who's going to present it?'

'Prince Charles.'

'Ooh … Getting to mix with royalty these days are we?'

Ross laughed. It made perfect sense though, as Prince Charles was the current Colonel-in-Chief of the Parachute Regiment. Once again I was a very proud father. At moments like that you suddenly feel very good about life in general. I couldn't wait for the chance to dress up in my glad rags and watch my son receiving his Afghan campaign medal from a member of the Royal Family.

Unfortunately, my happy anticipation of this event was certainly not matched by its smooth organization. Actually, it was one big cock-up – which makes you wonder if those organizing it really cared enough about what it might mean both to the soldiers themselves and their families. First of all Ross was told he would *not* be presented with a medal after all, because there weren't enough of the medals to go round. This certainly seemed odd to me. Then he phoned me again the day before the ceremony to say he would be presented with a medal after all. The soldiers were to be awarded individual medals bearing their name, regiment and serial number engraved around the rim. Not all the medals were actually received by the day of the ceremony; and on top of that, because of the sheer number of soldiers present, not everybody would be given their medal personally by Prince Charles.

Tanya and I drove up on the day, 2 December, to Merville Barracks in Colchester, where Ross was stationed and where the medal ceremony would take place. The security office was policed by a very young-looking soldier armed with an SA 80 rifle, and two civilian security staff.

'Morning, sir, how can I help you?' said one of the guards.

'We are here for the medal ceremony,' I said pointing to myself and Tanya.

'What's your name, sir?'

'Wynn.'

The security guard walked over to his mate in the security office to get him to check for our names on his list. He slowly shook his head in response.

'Sorry, sir. Your name's not on the list, I'm afraid.'

'My lad's in 3 Para and he's getting presented with his Afghanistan campaign medal this morning by Prince Charles,' I replied, somewhat exasperated.

'That may well be the case, sir, but your name's still not on the list,' he said, in a slightly patronizing way.

I was unsure what to do next. I suppressed my natural instinct to argue with the guy – I might risk not being allowed in at all.

'So look, how can we move this forward then, because we aren't really getting anywhere are we? – and there's a queue of cars behind me waiting to get in.'

'Have you got any identification on you at all, sir?'

'No, afraid not. Nothing at all.' I don't generally carry my Police Warrant ID card around with me. I wished I had that day.

'That doesn't really help matters at all now though, sir, does it?'

I felt pretty furious by now. On the one hand I knew he was only doing his job, but he also seemed to be intentionally unhelpful.

'What about if I phone my son and get him to come down here so that he can vouch for me?'

'He could be anybody sir. It still won't prove who you are, will it?'

'So you're telling me that if I phone my son to come here and ID me in front of you, that won't be sufficient to prove my identity?'

'Sorry, sir. Security. I'm sure you understand.'

Actually I didn't, but I thought I'd give it one more go before I reversed up and simply drove home.

'What about a credit card? My wife has a credit card on her,' I said, not even seriously thinking this would work.

The two security guards had a quick conversation between themselves about whether or not a credit card would fit the bill.

'OK, sir. That should be OK.' They both had to examine the card, of course, although I am not sure why. I had also thought about just saying 'bollocks' and driving on through. I quickly dismissed this idea when I realized that if I did they might actually open fire on me, mainly because of the imminent arrival of their very special guests, Prince Charles and Camilla Parker-Bowles.

'That's fine, sir,' the security guard said, handing me the card back. I was absolutely gobsmacked. After all that rigmarole, I couldn't believe we ended up getting into the barracks by showing my wife's credit card.

'Where do I go now?' I asked.

'Just follow the signs on the side of the road, sir,' he said turning away, seemingly glad to get rid of me. After I had passed about three road signs they suddenly ceased altogether, and I had to choose one road out of three at random. By now I was frustrated and very cold, and I just parked at the nearest possible location. There was nobody waiting about to show you where to go next, not a soul to direct you to the canteen to get a cup of tea to warm yourself up in the biting cold.

There were soldiers wandering about all over the camp, but nobody allocated to direct you. There was no board displaying relevant times and locations. Nothing.

Even allowing for the fact that Prince Charles was due to arrive for the medal ceremony shortly, and the Paras had a lot on their minds, I thought that the organization was absolutely abysmal. It was as if the families were a total irrelevance.

We eventually found our way to the Paras' canteen and managed to get a cup of coffee. Still no signs or anybody to tell us where to go or what time we had to be over at the parade square. After waiting in the canteen area for about 20 minutes, I told Tanya I was just going outside to see if I could find out what was going on.

It was a bitterly cold December morning – one of those days when the grass is solid with frost and exhaling a breath of air looks like you're smoking 20 cigarettes at once. There were Paras everywhere, but they did not seem to know what was going on either.

I stood just outside the main doors of the canteen building, stomping my feet on the ground in a poor attempt to keep warm. I had the collar of my thick, warm overcoat pulled up around my, by now, painfully cold ears, and my hands firmly in my pockets.

Then I saw a group of Paras all wearing their desert uniforms, with their traditional maroon berets, walking in my general direction towards the main doors of the canteen. By chance one of them was Ross.

'Hi, mate, how are you?' I said to him holding out my hand to greet him.

'Yeah, not too bad, dad. How's you?'

'Well, actually I am like an excited school kid,' I said, pulling the collars of my overcoat even tighter together in an effort to keep out the bitter cold. 'So, Ross, how's the day due to unfold then?' I asked, expecting him to know at least.

'I ain't got a clue, dad. I haven't got an effing clue what's going on. So far this morning we have been told that we are not being presented with our medals by Prince Charles, then we were told that we were, and now we have just been told that we aren't again; so if you know what's going on, you are a better man than me.' It was hard to grasp how an important occasion such as this appeared to be so badly organized.

Ross came into the canteen and showed Tanya and me his Afghan campaign medal. I was so proud of him and what he had achieved. The medal came in a black plastic case with the royal crown insignia engraved on the front of it. His name, regiment and personal military serial number were engraved round the rim.

At about 10 a.m., as if by magic, everybody just got up and started filing out of the canteen and heading off towards the parade ground for the beginning of the medal ceremony. Nobody had made an announcement, nor had anyone suddenly spotted some information. One person stood up and left, and everyone else simply followed – fortunately ensuring that we all arrived at the parade square on time.

All friends and family were asked to stand on the far side of the square, and then all of the soldiers marched on and took up a position on the opposite side. It started to get even colder, and as we had been standing there for about 20 minutes by now, the cold was even more noticeable. My toes were numb, my fingers were numb and my freshly shaved head was absolutely bloody freezing.

It didn't help the situation that we had the misfortune of having the family from hell standing right next to us. One of the kids thought it was an absolute hoot to keep bumping into one of my legs. The mother who must have seen what her child was doing only took an interest when eventually her brat tripped, fell over and banged his head. The younger of the two adult males thought it was absolutely hilarious, for some reason, to stand there and fart as loud as he could.

Prince Charles and Camilla Parker-Bowles finally managed to find their way to the parade square so that the royal salute could be given and the medal presentation could begin, somewhat drowned out for us by the three children talking, shouting and screaming their little heads off with no attempt at parental control. The medal ceremony seemed an irrelevance to them — I don't know why they bothered coming.

The royal helicopter landed on a grassed area no more than two hundred yards from the parade ground, yet for some reason it still took the royal party over 35 minutes to make the short journey there. Everybody by now was frozen. I at least could no longer feel either of my feet. I started getting bad chest pains as well, just for good measure.

Prince Charles took the royal salute, then presented medals to the walking wounded first — which included one young soldier who had been blown up by a booby-trapped sandbag, losing both legs and an arm. Although he had been wheeled onto the parade square by two able-bodied and very proud colleagues, once he had his medal pinned to his chest by his regiment's Colonel-in-Chief, he managed to summon up all his strength and actually walk slowly back to his waiting chair — an inspiring feat of personal bravery, and one typical of the regiment's ethos.

Everybody spontaneously stood to applaud this very, very brave young man and a few like me no doubt even had the odd tear or two in their eyes. My chest pains actually started when I saw him. I realized that, although I had seen such images many times before on the evening news and in national newspapers, I had never before seen such a thing in the flesh so to speak.

I stood looking at this poor, extremely brave man, and couldn't help thinking about Luke and his current trials and tribulations on military operations in Afghanistan at that moment. My chest pains started to get worse and my breathing was becoming more erratic. I knew that it was time to get out of there. So that's what I did.

I said to Tanya, 'Come on let's go, I'm not feeling too good at all.' We walked back to the car that I had parked just a short walk from the parade square, got in it and drove out of the camp and back down the A12 towards Basildon and home through a torrential downpour. As soon as I got in I went straight to bed. I didn't feel tired, but I thought if I could just lie down for a while and relax, my chest pains would subside.

I had been lying down for about an hour when my mobile rang. It was Ross.

'Hi, dad where are you?'

'At home in bed.'

'Yeah, all right, where are you really?'

'No. Honestly. I am at home in bed.' I said trying hard not to laugh.

'I've spent the last two hours freezing my nuts off. I am soaked through — and you ...'

'Ross, before you put your foot in it, mate, I had to come home as I'm really not feeling too good at all. I started to get chest pains and numbness down my left arm so I decided it was best I came home.'

'OK. It's a shame though, as you're missing out on the food they've laid on as well. Look, dad, I'll catch you later as mum and Joe and another of my mates are here.'

'That's nice for you. Look I am genuinely sorry that I couldn't stay till the end, but I started to feel really bad. I'll speak with you later. Enjoy the rest of your day.'

'Yeah, OK. Take it easy. Catch you later.'

Luke's award ceremony was six months later, in May 2009, ten days short of a year since Ross had first been deployed to Afghanistan with the Paras. At last it was all over and I could sit back and relax.

Ross was given time off by his Company Sergeant-Major so that he could attend Luke's medal ceremony at Bickleigh in Devon. Ross, Jon Burgess, a colleague of mine, and a friend of Luke's set off to attend it together. With our security pass clearly displayed in the front windscreen we were directed to a parking area on the other side of the road from the main barracks.

Besides the medal ceremony there was also a family fun-day going on until the afternoon, with bouncy castles, dodgem cars and rock climbing, but more importantly there was free food and beverages for all.

Ross looked resplendent in his number twos, finished off with a gleaming white belt, maroon beret, highly polished black boots and his Afghanistan service medal hanging proudly from his left breast pocket.

The three of us were patiently waiting to be let into the barracks along with the friends and relatives of some of the other Marines from 42 Commando. We were making small talk amongst ourselves to pass the time when a large group of Marines came marching down the main road that passed through the middle of the camp, before veering off to our right towards the astro-turf area to practise for their medal ceremony at 10 a.m. A few of the guys caught sight of Ross in his uniform and his immediately recognizable Parachute Regiment beret.

Together they then made a noise I can best describe as the sound of somebody about to be violently sick after a good night out on the town. Something like: WHUPPPP... It was an extremely funny moment, done in a very humorous manner. All three of us laughed, although Ross took his time before joining in. I asked Ross what the noise signified.

'As I'm sure you've worked out, the noise they were making was of somebody being sick. They were suggesting vomiting all over my beret,' he explained struggling to hold back his laughter.

A short while later Luke appeared at the main gates and there was a great deal of hugging, and handshakes all around. We had a quick chat and then Luke disappeared as he had to practise his march onto the parade square with the rest of his colleagues. A short while later the gates were opened and we were all allowed into the camp.

It was a glorious, hot and sunny day, without a cloud in the sky but with a slight breeze to help keep us all nice and cool. The three of us quickly found the NAFFI, and had a cup of coffee and a bite to eat.

The Marines decided to keep the day simple, so for them there was no important member of the Royal Family to take the salute and hand out the medals. Instead, their highest-ranked officer came to perform these duties – even if, like Prince Charles, he did arrive by helicopter.

The guys marched onto the square accompanied by music from the very smartly turned-out Royal Marines Band, their dark uniforms complemented by white helmets, gloves and belts.

Nobody could actually hear what the Commanding Officer said, as the microphone he was using didn't work. The only way I knew he had actually finished each stage of his speech was when everybody else around us started clapping. It didn't really matter too much to me if I am honest. I was there to support Luke and to enjoy what he had achieved.

The parade lasted about an hour. The members of 42 Commando trooped off the parade ground, resplendent in their green berets and desert-coloured uniforms. After falling out, they all gravitated back to where their families were waiting for them by the parade square. Just before Luke showed up I spotted an ex-colleague of mine from Basildon police station.

'Hi, mate, what are you doing here?' I asked.

'Exactly the same thing as you, Steve, I dare say.' We both laughed.

'I didn't know that you had a lad in the same mob as mine now.'

'Well, apparently so.'

Luke later showed us the memorial area – a peaceful location situated in the middle of the barracks between two of the accommodation blocks. The lawns were immaculately tended and looked like the tennis courts on the first day of Wimbledon.

There were two large memorial stones and a number of small trees that had been planted for each fallen comrade. Underneath each tree were polished metal plates bearing the name of the Marine and the location where he had fallen. There were wooden benches and blossoming trees dotted about the memorial area so that parents, wives, other close family members and comrades could come to the barracks by appointment and spend time with the memories of their loved ones.

A fine balance needed to be struck here. On the one hand it was only right and proper that colleagues and loved ones remembered their dead, yet nobody of course wanted to be reminded too often that a similar fate might await them. I must say that it was an extremely peaceful and pleasant area: the type of place where you could sit and eat a picnic, drink a cup of tea or simply read a book, on a warm spring day underneath a clear blue sky, with a gentle breeze blowing.

On a day like this you could remember the dead with some equanimity.

On the way home in the car, though, as Ross and Luke snoozed in the back, Jon told me the incredible story of his great-grandfather, Frederick William Owen Potts, who, at the age of only 22, won the highest possible honour – a VC – in the First World War. In August 1915, at Gallipoli in Turkey, Private Potts, although wounded in the thigh, remained for 48 hours under the Turkish trenches with another private from his regiment who was severely wounded and unable to move. He finally fixed a shovel to his comrade's equipment and, using this as a sledge, dragged the man over 600 yards back to safety, while under fire the entire way.

This brought it all back to me: both the inhumane horror of war and the extraordinary bravery of young soldiers risking their lives for each other. Both then and now, though, the question remained, as Harry Patch had articulated so forcefully: did we really know why we were sending our young men to face such danger, injury and death? Did it really serve a purpose?

7

Letters Home

Phone calls can be very frustrating and ephemeral – and it's hard to recall exactly what was said. The written word, on the other hand, has much more permanence – you can keep coming back to a letter and rereading it. This chapter therefore records some of the written words I received while my sons were in Afghanistan, and also passages from a regular and very helpful newsletter sent out by 42 Commando's commanding officer to keep families in the picture.

I will start, though, with the letter I gave to Ross the night before he first flew out to Afghanistan. I gave Luke a similar letter three days before he left.

Ross,

You are my son and I love you very much indeed. I am also very proud of you and what you have achieved with your life so far. The fact that you are reading this letter means that you are either already in or well on your way to Afghanistan.

The next six months will be extremely varied, and undoubtedly change and challenge your morals and views on life in general. The people you are there to help will not always want you in their country and sometimes will appear very hostile towards you; but stay focused.

You will see things that shock, scare, frighten, and yet also amaze you, all at the same time. You will laugh and you will cry. You will make great friendships and you will lose good friends; yet through all of this you must remain steadfast, firm and unwavering for your own well-being, and physical and mental survival.

There is every chance that you will see close friends injured or worse. Don't let this stop you forging ahead, doing your job to the best of your abilities and returning safely to your family and friends.

Be a rock for yourself and your comrades; be brave when you have to be, yet not foolhardy. Life is precious; it always has to be, especially when it comes to your own. Ask of yourself nothing that you would not expect from those who stand alongside you. Some of these men will become your brothers; remember that, and treat them accordingly.

The aim of any war is to kill the enemy and win a great victory for yourself, your comrades and your country. Identify your enemy quickly, aim true and shoot fast. Kill your enemy because if you give him the slightest opportunity he will try to kill you first and he will have no qualms about doing so. But when you have to kill, be swift and do it quickly, because there is no honour in making someone suffer when they are on the way to meet their Maker.

Remember your enemy is a man who like you has brothers, sisters, a mother and father, and maybe also a wife and children, and believes in his cause as much if not more than you believe in what you are doing. You don't have to like him, but give him the respect he deserves as a fellow warrior before and after you have dispatched him from this world.

One day you will have to answer to a Greater Being for your actions whilst on this earth. Make sure that when you stand before him you have nothing to reproach yourself for.

Although none of us, friends or family alike, can be with you in person on this particular journey, we are all with you in spirit and will be while you are away from us.

We are all very proud of you, and love you just as intensely. Keep safe and come home to us as you left us, and remember: it is better to be tried by twelve than carried by six.

Love,

Dad.

I was honoured and surprised — especially as the letter talks of death and killing — when a local priest I know, Reverend Ian Swift, asked to read it out to his congregation. He told me that someone came to him in tears afterwards, a veteran from the Second World War, and told him that the letter had taken him straight back to the middle of the last century when he too was fighting for his country in a war in a foreign land.

Yes, war is of course about death and killing, and death must be expected. My sons both left me their 'death letters' — a continual reminder, whenever I glanced at them, that whatever words they contained might be the last words I ever received from them.

In September 2008, when Ross had been back for about six weeks after his injury, I finally decided to open the letter. The previous week Ross had told me that no more guys from 2 or 3 Para, including himself, would be going out to Afghanistan for the rest of the current tour. So I knew that Operation Herrick 8 was finally over for Ross.

This letter had sat on my writing bureau for over four months, since the day before Ross left for Afghanistan. I had looked at it every single day while he was out there, wondering what was in it and hoping that I would never have to open it 'for real'. I had gone through a funny old routine of picking it up every day, turning it round 360 degrees before putting it back down about an inch away from where I had picked it up, then sliding it back to the position it had originally been in. I don't know why I did this. The only reason I can think of is that I did it once, then simply had to keep on doing it in case *not* doing it brought bad luck. Silly I know...

Here is the letter:

Alright Father!

As you're reading this, looks like the big man upstairs and 'Terry Taliban' proved us both wrong!

Bastards! Well, it's funny how life turns out and what paths we take.

I just wanted to write a couple of things in words as I never got a chance to say them to you again.

Firstly I love you from the bottom of my heart and I always will, you were one of my best friends and I loved spending time around you.

You taught me a lot about life and people and helped me through many situations.

I am very proud to be your son and when your time comes we will have a beer up here!

Keep being the father, husband and friend that you are to others, I'm just sorry we couldn't see each other again.

I know you said you would give the money to Luke, but I want you to enjoy a little bit of it, have a beer on me.

I'll be watching over you all
Love always, Ross!
Sorry

Ross later told me that the word 'sorry' was his apology to me for dying.

It was a truly remarkable and moving letter. I cried for two hours after reading it. It was funny yet sad; but what I really liked was its clarity and honesty. When somebody leaves you a death letter they have absolutely no reason to lie to you. This is their last chance to record how they saw their relationship with you.

Thinking about it now, it is a bit risky reading a letter like that because you do not know what it might contain. There could be a few home truths that you do not want to hear but, once you have read them, the long-term effect on your relationship might be irreversible.

I walked into work the next day feeling really good about myself, but after my second cup of tea and an hour spent going through my e-mails, I suddenly felt utterly overwhelmed by emotion. I couldn't concentrate, I couldn't even think straight. I knew it was time to get myself home. So I signed off, went home, and went to bed. I was

Alright father!

As your reading this looks like the big man upstairs and Terry Ellison proved us both wrong!
Bastards! Lol, its funny how life turns out and what paths we take.
I just wanted to write a couple of things in words as I never got a chance to say them to you again.
Firstly I love you from the bottom of my heart and I always will.
You was one of my best friends and loved spending time around you.
You taught me a lot about life and people and helped me through many situations.
I am very proud to be your son and when your time comes we will have a beer up here!
keep being the father, husband and friend that you are to others,
I'm just sorry we couldn't see eachother again.
I know you said you could give the money to Luke but I want you to enjoy a little bit of it, have a beer on me

I'll be watching over you all
Lae always Ross!

Sorry.

asleep as soon as my head hit the pillow. Five hours later I woke up sweating and feeling like I'd been hit by a train. What a roller-coaster of a journey it had been. I was amazed that reading a letter could have such an effect on me. Perhaps it was also all the months of stress and worry suddenly coming home to roost.

In March 2009, the night before I went to pick Luke up from Brize Norton on his return to the UK after he had been shot, I decided to open and read the death letter he had left me prior to his deployment.

Like the one Ross had left me, it had spent the previous six months perched on the top of my writing bureau in the living room. My reason for opening the letter now, and not waiting one more day, was simply over-excitement and the fact I knew that his war was now over. I guessed that with such a short time to go before the end of 42's deployment in Afghanistan, and the extent of his injury, there was absolutely no chance he would be sent back before the tour came to an end.

The front of the envelope was simply addressed 'Winnie'. The back of the envelope read, 'One step forward all those who haven't lost a son. Not so fast Wynn.' The letter itself, in true Luke style, ran:

Well I'm dead. Fucked that one up didn't I?

I'm going to keep this short as we've talked this over before. I knew the risks and I still played the game; it's big boys' rules so you've got to pay if you lose and I lost, that's all.

As a father you have done all that I could've asked for. You chided when necessary, advised on what you could, and always supported my choices. You never tried to live my life for me. You treated me as an adult and an equal man of my own right. In short, you got it right.

I've had my life but you've still got yours to lead, so crack on with it. Grieve, deal with the pain, but don't let it slow you down; don't let my choices slow you down. Be happy, live well. (Also, collect the three hundred pounds Ross owes me, and have a few drinks on my tab.)

Thanks for everything.

Love,

Luke

I still thank my stars that I never had to read either of these letters

09/09/08

WINNIE,

WELL I'M DEAD. FUCKED THAT ONE UP DIDN'T I? I'M GOING TO KEEP THIS SHORT AS WE'VE TALKED THIS OVER BEFORE. I KNEW THE RISKS AND I STILL PLAYED THE GAME; IT'S BIG BOYS' RULES SO YOU'VE GOT TO PAY IF YOU LOSE AND I LOST, THAT'S ALL.

AS A FATHER YOU HAVE DONE ALL THAT I COULD'VE ASKED FOR: YOU GUIDED WHEN NECESSARY, ADVISED ON WHAT YOU COULD, AND ALWAYS SUPPORTED MY CHOICES. YOU NEVER TRIED TO LIVE MY LIFE FOR ME: YOU TREATED ME AS AN ADULT AND AN EQUAL MAN OF MY OWN RIGHT. IN SHORT: YOU GOT IT RIGHT.

I'VE HAD MY LIFE BUT YOU'VE STILL GOT YOURS TO LEAD, SO CRACK ON WITH IT. GRIEVE, DEAL WITH THE PAIN, BUT DON'T LET IT SLOW YOU DOWN; DON'T LET MY CHOICES SLOW YOU DOWN. BE HAPPY, LIVE WELL. (ALSO, COLLECT THE £800 ROSS OWES ME AND HAVE A FEW DRINKS ON MY TAB.)

THANKS FOR EVERYTHING. LOVE

LUKE

for real. There are of course plenty of other parents who have had to, and will have to open such a letter in the worst possible circumstances.

As to 'life letters' rather than 'death' ones, below are some excerpts from letters I received from both my sons while they were on deployment. The first correspondence from Ross turned up in June 2008. There were two handwritten letters inside a Bluey (air-mail letter). By the time I got home from work, the airmail was lying on the hall floor half chewed by the dogs, who consider anything that comes through the door to be their rightful property. Luckily, the two letters inside were undamaged:

20 May

Salaamu Alaikum

That's hello in Pashtu. How's things? Sorry, couldn't really talk over the phone for security reasons: you know how it is! [...]

The first day I got here there were two rocket attacks on Kandahar airport. It was quite weird that the first thing I did, almost, was go to a funeral for a US Marine who got slotted by Terry Taliban. There were thousands of people there of all different nationalities.

Well look, I'm going to go because I want to get my fat one down. I love you lots and I'm another day closer to coming home. If you can write me back, would be good to hear from you! Say Hi to Tanya and the dogs from me.

Love, Ross

29 May

Alrite dad!

How's things? [...] Basically I am now out of Kandahar and at Camp Bastion, at a FOB (Forward Operating Base) called Inkerman. 40 Commando were there last time and they nicknamed it 'Incoming' because it got smashed so badly [...] Inkerman is a proper shit-hole, flooded, loads of people have gone down with it [diarrhoea].

I'm flying out tomorrow so all the fun and games will begin.

I've had to work in Bastion prison looking after Taliban, then did a 24-hour watch on a prisoner who had been shot. Been in one contact, didn't last for long but was buzzing.

[...] I've got R & R on July 18th and I'll be home for 14 days (2 days travel). Could you pick me up from Colchester because I need to get my stuff and take it home? I'll square you away when I get back. Look, I've got to go. I'll ring when I can. Love you loads. See you in a couple of months, OK!

Love from your son

Ross

P.S. Enclosed are a set of Wings I promised you!

These were a pair of desert Para wings, which miraculously the dogs had failed to chew to pieces. They'd fallen out of the envelope and found their way to safety underneath the front door mat. Seemed like a good sign to me...

On 13 June I heard again from Ross. The dogs chewed the letter again, but luckily it was still readable.

Alright Dad!

How's things? Happy Father's Day, hope you all had a good day with everyone around! How's Tanya and the dogs?

Weather out here is the same ... HOT.

We had environmental blokes here the other day and unsurprisingly we have the worst FOB of all the FOBs here in Afghanistan! Over 100 people going down with all sorts of lovely illnesses.

We had a two-minute silence for the 5 lads who died during the week; then the OC read out the paratroopers' prayer. Ironically enough, when I first got here, mail and choppers with supplies were scarce, then three lads from 4 Platoon died and we had loads of mail and supplies come in! It's funny how it takes three young blokes to die for everyone to give a shit about us! But anyway, that's life, and just got to crack on with things.

We used to get five 3-minute phone cards because we're in the worst place here and now they have decided to stop them because they've changed the tariff — yeah, cheers!

It's weird how the days go slow but fast here, if that makes sense. Can't wait to get home.

One of my pals who I passed out of depot with, was supposed to be going on R & R with me but got casevaced back home to the UK for heat exhaustion. Shame really because he was a good bloke and was helping me through this experience.

I'm keeping busy with patrols, stags, gym etc. Pretty sure I will look Ethiopian when I get back.

Been out here a month now. Time has flown by but I can't wait to get back home for good.

Look I'm going to go. Can you start sending me some parcels: sweets, crisps, pot-noodles etc. because I'm dying for some good grub. Can you also send some cans of Coke, Lilt etc.? Have you managed to get those long mits I asked for yet?

Anyway I'm off; I'll speak to you in about a week. Love you from the bottom of my heart. Speak soon, say Hi to Tanya and the dogs.

Ross!

The following was my 50th birthday card:

Dear Dad,

I just wanted to wish you a happy 50th birthday!

I wish I could be there with you and everybody else but unfortunately I can't.

Here enclosed is a little voucher and it has thirty pounds on it. Tanya said there was a T-shirt you wanted so there is enough here for you to get it.

I love you dad, more than most things in this world. I really hope our relationship doesn't end anytime soon!

You're one of my best pals and I'm proud that you're my old man, and Luke feels the same. I just wanted you to know.

I know things are hard but don't worry about me and Luke — we can look after ourselves out here. Just try not to worry too much.

I love you dad.

Have a great day and I'm sure Tanya will make it enjoyable.

Love from your two boys, Ross & Luke! xx

Generally I am a tough old boot, most definitely not a wilting wallflower, but I was certainly struggling to hold it together when I read what Ross wrote in the card. I think it hit me even harder because I knew he wouldn't be back till the end of October – if all went according to plan. With Ross back in Afghanistan after his R & R, I never quite knew if those words would turn out to be his last to me.

Luke's first letter from Afghanistan arrived in September 2008. I carefully pulled back the sticky sections of the Bluey to open it without tearing.

17/09/08

Alright Winnie?

I've been in Theatre for about five days, going through acclimatization and handover training. Soon we'll be relocating and cracking on with our first Op, closely followed by another one soon after that. I may be out of touch for a while.

For now though, we've found it mega-hot and difficult to operate in this weather and at this altitude. We're getting used to it and want to get to grips with the job.

I know I've not written much, but it's early days yet so not much to write about. I'll let you know as and when things happen.

Love,

Luke

As ever, Luke was short and to the point. His letter filled just over half a page. In fairness, he usually didn't spin things out unnecessarily if he didn't have much to say. If you got him on a topic he had a real interest in, though, you couldn't stop him talking for love or money! When he was younger, Luke, Tanya and I were driving to Thurrock one Saturday morning, and as we reversed out of the driveway, Tanya asked Luke a question about his passion, War Hammer. The journey took about half an hour. When we arrived he was still going, apparently oblivious to the fact that we had stopped listening to him some time ago...

October and November came and went with no more letters from him (though he phoned a few times). I was seriously thinking about popping down to the local bookies to see if they would let me place a bet on when he next wrote home!

Finally, in late December 2008 I popped down to the admin. department to check my post tray. There were a few things there for me, including a couple of Christmas cards. As I picked up the mail I noticed a blue airmail letter. I knew straight away who it was from – a nice surprise. As soon as I got back to my office I threw the rest of the mail into my in-tray and sat down at my desk to open the letter with slow, military precision. I peeled back the three sides of the Bluey without tearing it. I was impatient to read this letter from my son and full of expectancy to hear his news. But I burst out laughing. The letter was exactly six-and-a-half lines long:

17/12/08
Hi Winnie
Just a brief note. We're out on the ground soon enough and it looks to be quite tasty. It also looks like it is going to be an effing hang-out for a good few weeks.
Suffice to say, give my regards to everyone and have a good Christmas and New Year. Speak to you in 2009.
Love,
Luke.

I read it three times just to get my money's worth. I folded the letter up after reading it, leaned back in my chair, and went on laughing. But I suppose if I was chasing and fighting the Taliban all over

Afghanistan, writing letters in my down time wouldn't necessarily be at the top of my list of priorities.

Fortunately, to make up for Luke's scarcity of written words, throughout his deployment we received very helpful and informative newsletters from 42 Commando's CO, Lieutenant-Colonel Charlie Stickland. Strangely, this is not something that the Parachute Regiment did at all when Ross was serving in Afghanistan as part of Herrick 8, although both regiments did send out a booklet with much useful information about deployments and general welfare issues. But I still don't have a clue who the commanding officers were for either 2 or 3 Para during their deployment to Afghanistan. I am sure I could have found out, but that wasn't the point. There was never the same sense of belonging with the Paras as there was with the Royal Marines.

The newsletters were, I felt, a very good way to help families back home feel part of their son's deployment. You couldn't be there to fight for him, but you could help greatly by sending him out morale-boosting letters and parcels, and letting him know the family was thinking of him. In return, the newsletters kept you in the picture, as much as possible. In the first, Colonel Stickland outlined how important the continued support of friends and relatives was to his men. He explained that, as a father of three, he understood the pressures of being separated from loved ones whilst soldiers were away either on long training exercises or deployments in Afghanistan.

The bulk of 42 Commando, said Stickland, would form what is known as the Regional Battle Group (South) operating across southern Afghanistan. The terms of reference would be to conduct missions ranging from clearing Taliban safe havens to dominating an area that would ultimately facilitate the reconstruction of school and local facilities, and support the Afghan security forces, with the ultimate aim of self-governance by the people of Afghanistan. He reassured us that mitigating the potential risk to his men was very high on his operational planning agenda – but ultimately the Marines of 42 Commando were going to Afghanistan to do what they had trained and joined up to do.

The men of 42 Commando, he continued, would have to be like diplomats for their country and try to win the trust of the Afghan people. Their work would also see them involved in training the Afghan forces. This made their role extremely important.

Colonel Stickland also commented that families should not always believe everything they read in the press, some of which was inaccurate. He reassured families of the standard and quality of the kit and individual protective equipment that his men had been issued with.

All this sounded comforting and well organized. Unfortunately, of course, there is often a gap between intent and reality. The part of the newsletter about the regimental welfare department was slightly humorous to me. During Luke's initial training one of his grandfathers died. I phoned and spoke to the welfare department to ask if they could inform Luke of his death. They never did. I for one would take a lot of convincing about their reliability, though of course they have a hard task, especially during the Marines' deployment.

But in general the newsletter came across as very genuine – as though written from the heart and not just some generic piece of politically motivated rhetoric to appease us. Despite the ordeals the Commandos were undergoing, in subsequent newsletters Colonel Stickland usually managed to inject a little humour and also give a real feeling for what was going on – no mean achievement.

Here are some excerpts from the newsletters:

This latest excursion came under the banner of Operation Bor Barakai, meaning Great Thunder. We were tasked to interdict the Taliban in the Miribad Valley, an area that had never seen conventional troops. We were to degrade his stocks and weapons and explosives, and disrupt his command and control of the area.

We secured, cleared, searched and exploited each area that we had taken. Not a shot was fired but we detained those that gave us probable cause, found huge quantities of explosives and weapons and spent time talking to and understanding the local population. [...]

Our haul on this operation exceeded that of the last, and we are quickly making a name for ourselves amongst the international coalition here as an eager bunch of ferrets who can turn up a remarkable amount of information and hard evidence.

Our actions have been deemed a huge success: we significantly degraded the Taliban's capabilities but almost more importantly gained a deep understanding of this hitherto uncharted territory. It seems our work is providing a binding effect throughout the coalition as we develop our ability to lend our strengths to those who require or ask for it, be they Dutch, Canadians, Romanians or fellow Brits, and it appears the queue to work with 'Royal' is extending out of the door.

I hope this provides an insight into our activities. We are fighting for more phones and tents in Camp Roberts, so the lads have more contact and comfort. I'm also pushing hard for a clear date for our return. Key meetings to coordinate flights and flow of troops to take over from us will occur in mid-November, and as soon as I know, you will know. Our thoughts remain with you as we all push on through the tour.

The newsletter also included comments and notes from each of the individual companies. Luke's Lima Company notes included the following accounts, richly laced with humour:

Compounds, shacks, ponchos, vehicles, mosquito nets, grain stores, old blankets, bivvy bags, farmyards, courtyards, wet ditches, rooftops, orchards, ploughed fields, wheat fields, cannabis fields, soggy fields, and custom-made corn-on-the-cob storage areas. From arrival we've slept in, amongst and under them all.

Since lifting off from Exeter airport on 12 September 2008, Lima Company Group has been a busy lot. [...] Two Marines tried to jump a deep water-filled ditch, missed by an embarrassing distance, keeled over backwards and landed in the aforementioned water. Cheap raucous laughter all around. As darkness set over the first evening, one troop which shall remain nameless managed to mistake a latrine trench for the sentry trench. Fortunately, the long trail of tissues hanging off 8 Troops' miserable boots the following morning gave the game away. [...]

After 21 days living in field conditions, beards and moustaches had grown and a nondescript smell had accumulated, requiring several luxurious warm showers to clean. [...]

As the operation progressed, the Company moved from area to area following tip-offs and leads. One such move required crossing a fairly scary looking river. The all-terrain quad bikes were first to cross and did so through a mixture of driving, swimming, pushing and manhandling, a necessary evil as the bikes started to float downstream. This was prior to strong volunteers from 8 Troop acting as human pillars in the raging torrent, allowing the remainder of the Company to delicately tiptoe along the two-inch balance beam that comprised the bridge. Men with no sense of pride was pretty much the order of the night, as hands were held and shoulders, heads, rucksacks and rifles were used for balance. Clearly getting the best part of 120 men across wouldn't occur without incident.

What followed seemed to be lifted direct from a cheap comedy. Picture the scene: pitch-black, blindly shuffling one foot in front of another on an infinitely small bridge, wild hands groping for other firmer hands belonging to dark nameless bodies up to their midriffs in the fast-flowing water. Then a clipped yelp, slip and painful groan. One leg belonging to a Marine had inadvertently shot either side of the balance beam and as the full weight bore down a dull thud was audible. Wide, white eyes in the black night portrayed a sense of intolerable agony and the, 'I wish I hadn't done that' look. Matters worsened as he tipped sideways into the stream and was left to limp out of the water. The dull thud had been replaced by 30 men desperately trying to silence their instant hysterics. A tough 12 km yomp with full kit soon warmed up and dried out the remaining damp individuals.

As the operation continued we accrued a number of finds. These are improvised explosive devices and weapons caches of varying sizes and magnitude. Of particular note, Corporal Nick Bond's section made a fantastic find in a hay bale and were duly rewarded by maintaining a sentry and cordon around the hay bale overnight. As the rest of the Company found warm compounds to bed down in, 8 Troop slept in ditches and fields, rousing every couple of minutes to do push-ups, star jumps and grid sprints, trying to maintain a degree of warmth. I should mention at this point that it's starting to get quite cold at night. Needless to say, they were extremely proud custodians of their find. [...]

The humorous warmth of these anecdotes, combined with a sense of the tough ordeals the Marines were undergoing, was vividly conveyed in such passages. Every time one of these newsletters arrived, I couldn't wait for the next to turn up. I was like an excited little kid. They almost made me feel I was there myself.

Naturally, humorous quips were not always the order of the day. In the next newsletter, Lt.-Colonel Charlie Stickland had the unenviable task of informing us all about the sad death of two of the guys — two of *his* guys. He didn't want to lose anybody, although realistically he knew the chance of getting through a seven-month tour of Afghanistan without suffering casualties and fatalities was very remote:

I sat down to scribble my monthly thoughts to you, upbeat following another hugely successful operation by the bulk of the unit acting as the Regional Battle Group South (RBGS), and knowing that J Company in Helmand and Kabul are doing an absolute cracking job. However my mood and tone has shifted following the tragic events of but two days ago.

We have lost two of the 'Smiley Boys' of 42 Commando: Marine Tony Evans and Marine 'Geordie' Sparks were operating with their comrades in Juliet Company in a place called Nad-e-Ali, which is just outside the Helmand provincial capital of Lashkar Gah. [...] The boys were on patrol when they were engaged by the enemy. The patrol's reactions were hard and fast and absolutely correct, with Marines Evans and Sparks providing fire support for their colleagues; and in doing so they tragically lost their lives. We can only take solace from the fact that they were fighting shoulder to shoulder with their fellow 'Jesters' in Juliet Company, doing the job they both loved and thrived on. I also remain convinced that we are making a difference, albeit with small and difficult steps. [...]

Intelligence feeds had brought to our attention a number of compounds of interest, where insurgent weapons and bomb-making facilities might potentially lurk. Our mission was to interdict the insurgent safe havens of the district to degrade Taliban capabilities and his longer-term perception of security, and so as ever our planning process whirred into action to decide how best to go about that task. [...]

Over the first 24-hour phase of the cycle, Kilo Company had a significant success in the form of a fully functional IED factory, which revealed an array of prepared explosives and many more in constituent parts. As a result, over 600 kg of explosive and many weapons have now been removed from the area which will not now threaten us, our ISAF colleagues or the local population. There is no more demonstrable way of illustrating how the boys are making this area a safer place for all.

Lima Company also had success with another haul of ammunition and weapons and we took a number of detainees with associated evidence, several of whom are now facing prison sentences. Additionally, each time the insurgents took the Commando Recce Force on, they were rapidly and robustly dispatched.

Throughout these periods of movement and compound searching it was clear that the insurgent just could not respond quickly enough with any sort of coherent challenge, and this is what I mean when I say that I always seek to stack the odds in our favour. Rapid manoeuvre and the lads' own outstanding professionalism and cultural awareness have so far proved a recipe for success which we aim to exploit throughout this tour.

The training we conducted over the summer, while painful from a family point of view, is paying dividends, undoubtedly keeping us as safe as possible in this environment. At the most grass-roots level the Commando Group is doing you and itself proud. Intelligent posture and keen interaction with the local population is setting us up for continued success as they learn that the Commando flashes we wear signify an improvement to their lot. In all that we do it is essential we are seen as balanced, honourable warriors who are fair, straightforward and targeted in our actions.

I am constantly aware that the flow of information back to you is crucial for your ongoing support and situational awareness, and I hope to offer you a Company-wide set of articles and pictures in December. However, I have no idea how long our next operation is going to be. I hope this short offering from me suffices in the meantime.

He was absolutely spot-on about the flow of information coming back to us being crucial. It certainly stopped me from going insane on many an occasion. The newsletters turned up with some regularity – and certainly far more frequently than anything from Luke. I almost started to believe that I wasn't hearing anything from him because he had managed to get himself lost and his officers simply hadn't realized he was missing yet!

The next newsletter arrived on Christmas Eve:

[...] Well, it finally happened, the rain has come. Two days of torrential rain and the building site we are in has turned into a swamp. There are scenes here reminiscent of 1917, hollow-eyed but focused men, digging trenches, improvising shelter, full of banter and covered in mud. You will be pleased to hear a miniature Christmas tree sits in the middle of the compound courtyard where we now reside.

The boys are working hard, there is nothing short and sharp about this operation, we are going to be in the field for some time [...]

Hopefully as many people as possible will have the time to get one of the welfare satellite phones to ring home on 25 December. However, I must warn you, 42 Commando Group will be working on Christmas Day. Our Christmas is going to be delayed until we return to Kandahar where we intend to have a Unit Christmas lunch and rip into the piles and piles of parcels that are waiting for us, as we haven't managed to get them forwarded to us in the field. Letters do get through when helicopters are available.

By the time you all read this letter, the jungle drums will have been beating about our recent three casualties. Thankfully they are all doing well and the casualty evacuation chain has remained second to none and the high-tech hospital in Camp Bastion is absolutely brilliant. All are well, and their recovery looks assured.

Separation is hard, especially at Christmas time. Think of us covered in mud, a bit tired but smiling and full of spirit. You are in our thoughts and I know we all wish we could be with you at this special time. Many of us will tick Christmas off as another tour milestone. Christmas, then R & R and then we are nearly there. [...]

Best wishes and seasons greetings to you all from muddy Helmand.

The next newsletter I'll quote from arrived in late January:

[…] Once again this was a truly expeditionary operation for the Commando Group. As the gypsies of southern Afghanistan we negotiated Kandahar City once more and ran all our vehicles down to Camp Bastion. We set up home in a 12 × 12 tent and the boys camped in the overflow tents.

We disrupted and interdicted the enemy, with all sub-units in heavy contact as we surprised and unbalanced significant groupings of insurgents on our intersection. Our next task was to secure and establish two patrol bases; this involved the Herculean task of constructing a route under fire to get the stores in, brave engineers building under withering enemy fire and the Company's pushing the enemy back some 2.5 km. […]

The Commando's Group efforts have made a significant contribution to the overall Nad-e-Ali security plan, success borne out of the robustness and endurance of the Marine. Our time in Nad-e-Ali was not without its difficulties. Our first experience of the Afghan monsoon created scenes reminiscent of the Somme or Glastonbury (without cider, welly-boots or Kylie Mynogue). We have suffered losses of Cpl. Rob Deerings (attached to us from CLR) and LCpl. Ben Whatley (Lima Company), Marines Tony Evans and Georgie Sparks – for whom we have taken moments to absorb, remember and move on before we can remember again when we link up with the families of our comrades on our return to the UK in April. […]

Before I sign off, two further points. Firstly, I know you would like a little bit more granularity and detail from Company level, and we will endeavour to satisfy this requirement when we all tumble back from R & R. Secondly, I am duty-bound to right a wrong. Last weekend an article appeared in the *News of the World* about Operation Red Dagger, making the claim that the Black Knights of Kilo Company fought the tenacious battle for Zarghun Kalay. On behalf of the men of Lima Company, I must correct this, for the credit must go to Lightning Lima Company for taking Zarghun Kalay.

That last paragraph was particularly satisfying for me to read, as Luke was a member of Lima Company. Not only did he actually take part in the battle for Zarghun Kalay, but his photograph appeared twice in the *News of the World* article. His letters may have left something to be desired – but not his brave actions. And what I desired more than anything – certainly more than his words – was his safe return.

Over these seven months I had really looked forward to receiving the periodic newsletters from Luke's CO in Afghanistan. I got to recognize names of places that I had never previously heard of, and even learned a few words of Pashtu.

The final newsletter of the tour was waiting amongst the bundle of mail on my writing bureau when we returned from our holiday in Tenerife in April 2009. It included comments by the Brigade Commander:

[...] As we enter the last few weeks of the Op Herrick 9 tour, and thoughts turn to the homecoming and beyond, I thought it might be useful to give you my thoughts on what we have achieved so far on the tour.

By any measures, this has been an extremely successful and rewarding tour, and everyone I speak to feels justifiably proud of what we have achieved. Despite opposition from a very determined foe, we have succeeded in pushing back Taliban influence in areas that have not seen security for some time. This has allowed encouraging progress to take root across the province, and the growing number of newly opened shops, schools and clinics is a telling indication of returning normality in areas that have long been without hope. The provincial governor has been able to conduct outreach meetings in areas where insecurity has precluded his attendance in the past, and the recent voter registration operation passed largely without incident in Helmand. For the first time, the Afghan Government has been able to access outlying districts and have a real impact amongst the local population. Other measures of success are the notable progress we have made in training the Afghan National Army and the Afghan Police, and the degree of disruption we have created within the narcotics community in Helmand. In addition, reconstruction projects are springing up around the province, including road building, new police stations and mosques, electricity distribution and agricultural development projects. This level of activity would have been unthinkable only months ago and could not have taken place without the endeavour and sacrifice of the troops on the ground in providing the necessary security.

This is but a snapshot, but I hope it gives you a feel for the depth and diversity of our achievements over the tour, each building on the efforts of our predecessors who set us up so well. I also hope that it provides a balancing view to the less-than-positive media reporting that you often receive in the UK. It will not surprise you that your loved ones are performing superbly in extremely challenging and uncomfortable circumstances. Every day, they are putting their lives on the line, behaving proportionately despite extreme provocation, and always acting with the well-being and interests of the local Afghan people at heart. Everyday I am in awe of their professionalism.

But such success has not been without tragedy, and many good friends and fine soldiers have lost their lives with many more seriously injured. We are profoundly touched by this, and our thoughts frequently turn to those who have lost loved ones on this tour, or who are struggling to overcome injury. Yet I have met no one here who has allowed their sorrow to deflect them from their unerring determination to succeed. Those we have lost would expect nothing else from us, and we owe it to them to maintain such focus through to the end of the tour and beyond.

In closing, I want to thank you all, the friends and families of Op Herrick 9, for your unwavering support throughout the tour. Your courage, patience and strength have been deeply appreciated by us all, and have been a major source of morale in difficult times. As you read above of our many successes, I hope you recognize that this has been a team effort in which you yourself have played no small part.

Brigadier Gordon Messenger RM
Commander Task Force Helmand

It was strange to think that this was the last newsletter, and that most of the Marines were now safely home. My thoughts were inevitably also with the families of the guys who didn't manage to make it back and the many, many more who had been seriously injured. These were all just young men simply doing the job that they had been trained to do. The price for them and their loved ones was very costly.

Of course, it may have been a price ultimately worth paying for the peaceful future of a whole country – which is certainly what Brigadier Gordon Messenger suggests above. Writing this a year later, though, in March 2010, the picture in Afghanistan no longer seems quite as straightforward as the Brigadier suggests. News comes thick and fast – almost on a daily basis – of terrible casualties and fatalities amongst Nato forces, with no end in sight to this apparently intractable or even insoluble conflict. Is it all worth it? That, as they say, is a question beyond my pay-scale. As the Brigadier suggests, we doubtless owe it to the dead and injured to see this through, if possible, to a successful conclusion. Whether it is possible is another question...

8

How Was It For Them?

I decided this book would not be complete without getting both Luke and Ross to answer some questions about their own experiences.

I asked Ross first. At the time he had been back from Afghanistan for just over six months. He had had his ups and downs since he returned to the UK. Due to the back injury he sustained on tour, his military status had been downgraded. This meant that to be upgraded again for front-line duties he had to be passed fit by the Company's doctor, undergo an arduous physical test and then finish off with an eight-mile timed run.

At the end of February 2009, Ross was due to go to Oman for six weeks with his platoon for some very tough and demanding training, but because the doctor wouldn't upgrade him without him passing all the required tests, he was told at the eleventh hour that he couldn't go. I don't think Ross was best pleased about this. He still wanted to feel part of his unit, though his time in Afghanistan had affected him quite badly and he most certainly wasn't looking forward to returning for a second tour. He wasn't in any kind of rush to get his back sorted out, and to be honest I believe that he was hoping it would be a lot worse than it actually was so that he could get out of the Army – but it wasn't to be.

He went away on a week's off-road driver training in Aldershot, hoping he could get a transfer to the regiment's vehicle maintenance section – which didn't happen. He enjoyed himself while he was down there and came back with renewed vigour, deciding he was going to knuckle down, get stuck in and see out the remaining two and a half years of his time as well as he could.

We sat down together at the dining-room table with a cup of tea. I switched on the tape recorder and began the interview.

What was your most memorable moment in Afghanistan? (I really wasn't sure how Ross was going to answer this one, but I did laugh at his response.)

Eh, probably flying home to be honest, he said, almost without thinking.

What was your worst memory or scariest moment whilst you were in Afghanistan?

One of them was when we went out on patrol and three lads got blown up by a suicide bomber and we were sitting in the FOB and the Brigade Commander came in and gave us some brilliant speech about how he knows what it was like to lose blokes. The whole atmosphere, everyone was down – and even though you might not know them, it still brought tears to your eyes.

When one of the snipers was shot we were running across open ground and the rounds were whizzing past my face. My heart stopped beating and to be honest I thought that I was going to die. I suppose it was pretty scary.

Listening to Ross it was clear that he was vividly reliving the incidents as he described them to me.

Was your kit, including weapons, radios and vehicles good enough for the job?

When we went out on patrol we didn't need vehicles as such.

What about your radios and weapons, though?

Obviously there's a limited amount of kit out there. You are trained to use the weapons that you have. The weapon is only as reliable as its user. The kit usually does the job that it's intended to do.

When we were carrying the ECM (Electronic countermeasure), which was a really heavy piece of kit, we never came into contact with any IEDs. Well we did come into contact with IEDs, but the ECM didn't really help. I just felt that it was a useless, heavy weight that was an absolute waste of time. You could be carrying lots of other kit that was useful to both you and your mates.

Did you have the job of carrying the ECM when you were out on patrol with your mates?

When you are out there the new bloke always gets to carry the ECM, that's just the way it is.

Just explain for me if you can what the ECM actually is. What does it do?

Basically it puts a 40-metre radius around your call sign and your blokes. It will then let you know when an IED is within that distance. If the ECM starts to bleep then you all start walking very slowly and start looking round for fresh ground disturbance that could indicate a possible IED. You also start looking for something that doesn't look to be part of the natural landscape, like a pile of rocks that have no reason to be where they are.

You never go further than 20 metres without stopping. You don't touch anything that doesn't need touching. If you see an enemy weapon lying on the ground you leave it where it is and don't even think about picking it up just in case it's booby-trapped.

Do you think that the tactics you were asked to employ were generally the correct ones?

Em, well that's the thing, you never know where the enemy are, but when you get opened up on during a contact you do what you've got to do and hope that your basic drills get you through it, with of course a lot of good fortune from lady luck.

Did your pre-deployment training prepare you sufficiently for your actual deployment in Afghanistan?

Well, because I didn't finish my training and pass out from depot until April 2008 and the regiment had already deployed to Afghanistan in March, I didn't get any pre-deployment training. My training as such was out on the ground in Afghanistan – but I'll tell you one thing, you certainly learn effing quickly that way.

We had about a week's input about what type of weapons the Taliban use and what type of IEDs they deploy and how they construct them. To be honest you can do all the training in the world but when you are getting shot at your training from Depot kicks in and you do what comes naturally to you.

Do you think militarily our involvement in Afghanistan will actually make a difference?

They are going to be out in Afghanistan for the next 15 to 20 years regardless of what I did and what I was a part of during my tour out there. Afghanistan has been continually invaded over the last few centuries by some of the best armies in the world, and the country has seen them all off.

I think overall the British Army does, has made and will make a difference; but no, I don't think that I personally made a difference to what's eventually going to happen in Afghanistan. I did my duty to the best of my ability, that's all I know. You will always have casualties in war and some of them will be fatalities. Do their families think their loved ones' involvement was worthwhile? I'm not sure how they would answer that one.

When you were on the front line fighting for your lives, did you and your colleagues ever discuss or concern yourselves with the politics of why you were there?

All that politics and bullshit goes out of the window. We signed on the bottom line. You know that you are going to have to go to Afghanistan. You do your training and you go and fight – and yeah, it's exciting, but that soon wears off. I suppose it's like you being a copper and never nicking anybody or being a fireman and not having gone and dealt with a fire. No, we never discussed politics because we weren't there because of that. As far as we were concerned we were simply there doing our job.

Would you look forward to going back to Afghanistan? (I had a good idea what Ross's answer was going to be to this question.)

From my personal experience, I would have to say no. If there is such a thing as hell on earth, then that place would be Afghanistan. But you could speak to different regiments who weren't out on the front line and they might have a different perspective on it and give you a different answer.

What has this experience taught you about yourself?

Personally I wouldn't say that it's taught me anything about myself that I didn't already know before I went out there. No.

Has your experience in Afghanistan changed you at all?

When you come back, at first everyone claps their hands and says well done, but that's very short-lived. When something good happens everyone jumps on the bandwagon. But if you mess up somehow, everybody looks down their nose at you.

Maybe your friends and family understand what you went through a bit, but not the general public, no. At the end of the day we are the buffer between good and evil, a necessary evil.

What was your understanding of why you were sent to Afghanistan?

Well, my understanding [laughter] was that I went there because I was told to, period. I had read up on what Afghanistan was all about, where it was and some of its history, but no, we weren't sat down by our bosses and given the low-down about why we were going out there.

Would you recommend a life in the military to your friends at all?

Being in the Army does teach you a lot and how to look after yourself. You can learn different trades which you can then use in civvy street. Personally it's not for me, but I can see that some people would enjoy it and get a lot out of it. I suppose it's swings and roundabouts really.

While you were away, what was the luxury from back home that you missed the most?

Cold water was the luxury I missed the most. Where we were we had to drink out of a well, and to clean it they added chlorine and it tasted horrible. It was 40 to 50 degrees most of the time, and water was something that you needed big time in that heat. The colder the better. Yes, a cold bottle of water most definitely. Right is that all?

Yes. That's it. We are all done.

We shook hands, and smiled at each other.

I sat down with Luke on the Sunday evening after he returned from Afghanistan and asked him exactly the same questions. It was interesting to see how his answers differed.

OK, first question then.. What was your most memorable moment from your tour of Afghanistan?

Well, like the saying goes, war is 95 per cent boredom, sitting around just waiting, and then 5 per cent of extreme moments of excitement. A lot of the tour was very hard going but then sometimes it could also be very monotonous as well. Sometimes that all just seems to roll into one. The edges get blurred between the two. You will have the odd contact or operation where things are really tasty. Out of all of those contacts and operations none of them sticks out more in my memory than any of the others.

OK, thanks for that. Could you just explain to me exactly what it is you mean when you use the word 'contact'.

Yeah, sure. A contact is where you and the enemy interact with each other, where there is an exchange of gunfire. Basically a scrap with guns and weapons.

What was your worst or scariest memory in Afghanistan?

Well, funnily enough it was most probably the first contact I was involved in. We had been on the ground for only a few weeks on a vehicle-borne operation when, whilst driving along in a convoy, the tenth vehicle in the convoy was blown up by an IED and thrown on to its side. It was only about four vehicles ahead of the vehicle I was driving. It wasn't that bad actually and none of our guys were killed although one of the lads was quite seriously injured. Another of the guys had part of his hand blown off and there were two other lads who were also injured, with minor fractures.

Looking back on it now we had many more dangerous contacts than this during the tour, but I suppose because it was the first one I was actually involved in, it is the one that I will always remember the best.

Even though there were some experienced guys in our section who had been involved in earlier tours in Afghanistan and Iraq – which ensures that you have support and direction at such times – that doesn't stop you from freezing, and if I am honest I froze at first. The question What do I do? was ringing round inside my head. What I mean is that at first I didn't instinctively react to what was going on around me, but as soon as

I heard somebody screaming out for a medic, I grabbed hold of my first aid kit, as I am one of our section's medics, and ran off to see what I could do to help.

Hell, Luke. Let me get this right, now. Some of your mates are injured in an explosion, two of them relatively seriously, and they then see you running towards them to offer first aid. I'm surprised they didn't feign death, I said laughing.

Yeah, very funny. Anyway, thankfully the two guys that I got to weren't that badly hurt. I managed to get them away to a nearby ambulance and did my job before returning to my vehicle.

OK, next question. Was your kit, including weapons, radios and vehicles good enough for the job that you were tasked with doing?

Mmm ... that's a two-part answer really. If there's a certain bit of kit that we needed for operational purposes, our bosses would do their damnedest to make sure that we got it and that the powers that be will find the money to provide it. Certainly this was true for bits of kit such as night-vision equipment, thermal imagery kit, and encrypted radios – which are a massive improvement on the basic kit – and ballistic glasses.

All of our weapons had been upgraded with little 'Gucci' extras such as forward hand grips. A lot of us also had upgraded laser sights. Yeah, our weapons and kit were all spot on. First class. I even had a pistol, an up-to-date new 9 mm Sig.

The vehicles and body armour were a totally different kettle of fish, as was our electrical warfare equipment, but I'm not going to talk about it for restricted security reasons.

The body armour was far too heavy. The plates were too bulky and could have been a lot thinner. What was really annoying is that there are much better plates in existence, but they (Ministry of Defence – MOD) won't buy them. The Osprey set that they provide you with is atrocious. I don't actually think that it is fit for purpose. I know that one of our lads died when the vehicle that he was travelling in was blown up by an IED. The explosion didn't kill him. It was the armour plate in the front of his body armour. It flew out of its pouch, caught him on the jaw and broke his neck.

These plates that the MOD provide cost between £1000 and £1200. A warrior plate-carrier costs about £900 but we couldn't wear them because of Health & Safety rules. Now isn't that just absolute, utter bollocks?

The helmets weren't much better either. They are extremely heavy and cumbersome and actually restrict your vision. OK, they will stop a 7.62 round, but yet again there are much better bits of kit on the market that do the job just as well, like the ones you saw the Special Forces guys with when you picked me up from Brize Norton.

The thing that struck me most about Luke's response to this question was the passion and the annoyance in his voice. He wasn't just having a moan. You could tell that he genuinely believed that the guys should have had the best kit available and he didn't think they had.

OK, mate. Tactics next. Were the tactics that you were asked to employ generally the correct ones?

When I was doing my initial training at the CTC (Commando Training Centre), down at Lympstone, like all of the guys I was trained to a very high standard. I have no problem with that. In fact I would go as far as to say that the Royal Marines have the best possible military training in the UK, if not in the world. OK I know that I am biased and that Ross wouldn't necessarily agree with that, but you can't get much better and that's a fact, Jack.

However, the one big problem was that out on the ground we couldn't actually use that training. We had to do a hell of a lot of night-time reccies [reconnaissance] in readiness for a daytime attack the next day. We would send out eight-man teams. Usually four of the guys would sit up at an agreed location, whilst the other four guys would move forward to the target location, quite often without most of their kit on – their helmets, body armour and day sacks – so as to allow them to move with stealth and speed and to simply be a lot more mobile.

The main reason for doing it in this way was because bigger teams mean shedloads more kit, which in turn means much more noise, which means more chance of being heard and discovered, which ultimately means more casualties – which the hierarchy most definitely do not want.

We weren't allowed to get on and do our job on the ground, the job that we have been trained to do, which made things very frustrating and difficult for us.

Sounds like politics play a big part in it.

That's a hell of an understatement.

Unlike Ross, when you passed out from Lympstone you had plenty of time to do your pre-deployment training. Looking back on it now, do you think you were sufficiently prepared for your actual deployment in Afghanistan?

I think that I would have to say that our pre-deployment training was as accurate as it was possible to get. Briefings from guys who hadn't actually been deployed to either Iraq or Afghanistan, but who were simply reading the information from reports, didn't help things at all. To my mind that gave them a total lack of credibility. We were however very well trained in the use of all of the weapons that we would possibly have to use in Afghanistan, as well as the weapons the Taliban are known to use.

The Black Watch are taking over from us and my understanding is that they haven't had the same extensive training that we were given, which I must say I find totally unbelievable.

Do you think that our military involvement in Afghanistan will ultimately make any difference whatsoever?

Well, that's a question way above my pay-scale. You would need to ask somebody of at least officer level, if not higher, who is in possession of the much wider picture that we are only a microcosm of. At the end of the day I am on the ground doing the job of a basic rifleman.

We do make a difference, I suppose, and we could make even more of a difference. But we continually have to wait for confirmation of our actions from much further up the food chain. This includes even very basic military decisions. This eats up too much valuable time and leaves the guys feeling very frustrated.

We operated all over the place and not just at the FOBs. Our presence is making a difference in Afghan. Helmand is much more difficult because we simply need more troops so that we can clear the Taliban from a location. At the moment we will gain a location but then lose control of it just as quickly once we have left. We will then have to have the same fight again to try and regain it, which has led to avoidable casualties and fatalities.

Did you or any of your colleagues sit round and discuss the politics of why you were actually in Afghanistan?

Yet again, that's way above my pay-scale to worry myself about stuff like that. I was busy enough just doing my job to even think that deeply about politics, even if I wanted to and, believe it or not, I didn't.

Now that you have completed a tour — well, nearly managed to complete a tour — would you want to go back to Afghanistan again?

You do six months in a shit-hole like that and then come and talk to me; and I did actually do six months, as we went out there a month early.

And your answer to this question was, Luke?' I said, grinning.

I wouldn't go back to Afghanistan as a bog-standard Marine. There are too many restrictions on you at that level. I would definitely go back in some kind of specialist role though, like BRF or SFSG, because you get much better kit; and let's just say that you are allowed to operate without so many restrictions on you.

What has your experience in Afghanistan taught you about yourself?

Nothing I could actually pinpoint. I went out there to do a job and I did it. I would like to think, like we all do I suppose, that I did it to the best of my ability. Yeah, OK, you see and do things that are a bit out of the ordinary and that most people would never even have to think about let alone have to do, but I don't feel that it has changed me in any way. I won't necessarily forget certain things, that's for sure, but there have been no changes, no.

To most people back home you are seen both as a hero and a warrior. Do you see it the same way at all?

No not at all. As far as I am concerned I was simply doing my job to the best of my ability. I'm not a hero. The heroes are the ones who didn't make it back, as far as I am concerned. They paid the ultimate price, the highest price that anybody could ever pay. They paid with their lives. In my book that makes them real heroes. Like most of the guys out there I had a pride and a self-belief in what I was doing and, more importantly I suppose, in what I was a part of. If that makes me a warrior, then yeah, I will accept that, but don't call me a hero.

What was your understanding of why you were sent out to Afghanistan?

We were never sat down and given a politically driven speech about the reasons why Britain actually had troops in Afghanistan, if that's what you mean. We were told what we were going to be doing out there from a military, tactical point of view, but that was about as heavy-going as it got. There was no political claptrap about hearts and minds stuff.

Would you recommend a life in the military to any of your friends at all?

I have spoken with some of my mates about my experiences whilst I was in Afghanistan – but only those who have asked – mainly because that is the end result of all the training I did. In the current financial crisis that most people find themselves experiencing, there are worse jobs that you could be doing. It has certain perks attached to it. It's not too bad a job – reasonably well paid, and a good pension at the end of it. I wouldn't necessarily try and sell it to my friends, but then again I wouldn't be trying to dissuade them from joining the corps either.

When you are thinking about joining they most definitely try and sell it to you by glamorizing it somewhat, and downplay the bad bits. I would certainly let anybody thinking of joining the Marines know just how hard the initial training is, both physically and mentally.

While you were away serving in Afghanistan, what was the luxury from back home in the UK that you missed the most?

I don't think there was anything in particular that I missed. As you know, a lot of the work that I was involved in meant that I was out on the ground for long periods of time, but when I got back to the KAF

(Kandahar Airfield) I had everything that I needed. I certainly had a very good standard of living whilst I was back at base.

There you go then. I just really wanted to know from you at first hand what it was actually like doing the job that you were expected to do in Afghanistan.

Actually, I quite enjoyed it. Not as bad as I thought it was going to be.

OK, mate, I know that you have told me about the incident when you were actually shot, but can I just go through it with you again whilst I have got you, so that this time I can record your answers?

Yeah, no trouble, mate. I was out and about on an operation called Abbi Tooray. I won't go into any details about what the operation was all about or exactly where it was, but I can say that we were also looking for IEDs, drugs, cash and weapons. For the first part of the operation things had been relatively quiet and we had not come into contact with the Taliban. We had swept through the area that we were in totally unopposed.

The area contained an old fort from way back. We had some up-to-date intel that the Taliban were trying to build up their numbers in the area and re-arm themselves. As well as the old fort there were other compounds that surrounded it. It was strange when you were searching compounds, because part of you wanted them to be empty and totally devoid of anybody – that way you didn't have to sit there thinking about which, if any of them, were Taliban and which were simply frightened friendlies. If they were empty then you also had to consider that might be because the Taliban were in the area and the locals had gotten the hell out because they knew an attack was coming.

Earlier in the day there had already been two failed suicide bombing incidents, in which all the bastards had managed to do was to blow themselves up and thankfully not any of our guys.

We started sweeping our way through the different compounds and getting nearer and nearer to the old fort towards the south-east corner of the main compound. My troop had just started clearing a pumping station so that we could get some arcs onto the fort. The time was around the 10 a.m. mark, when all of a sudden we were engaged by the enemy –

not from the fort where we were expecting it, but south-east and south-west of our location.

There was a burst of incoming enemy machine-gun fire directed at us from about two hundred yards away, which was pretty close. The enemy were using 7.62 mm rounds of ammunition, and they have a maximum range of around four hundred metres. You wouldn't want to get hit by one of them. Add to that they are five inches long and travel at 2300 feet per second, you quickly get the idea of how potentially lethal these bullets are. We returned fire, but that only seemed to piss them off even more. The rate of incoming fire only increased and was getting closer and closer to where we were.

I'd just entered one of the ruins and was by the wall on the eastern side of the building. Straight across from it was another wall only a matter of yards away. I peeled over to this other wall so that I could start putting out effective arcs of fire towards the enemy's position on the eastern side of the ruins. I was trying to get myself into a good firing position, and as I did this the incoming fire that had been going over our heads suddenly dropped and started hitting the western wall to the right of the room I was in.

As these rounds started hitting the wall, I felt a pain in my left shoulder, which felt like somebody whacking me with a cricket bat. I had always thought that if I were ever to get shot it would feel more like a sharp stabbing pain than anything else.

I thought it was a ricochet I had been hit by. I didn't think for one second that I had been shot. I thought it was just a bit of brick or mortar that had been shot away from the wall. It didn't actually feel how I imagined it would. As I said, it felt more like a blunt whack.

When it hit me the power of it was so strong that it spun me around. I dropped my rifle, and then fell to the ground. I was in a bit of pain and shocked but not 'in shock', if that makes sense.

There were a couple of my muckers in the same room as me when I was shot. One of them shouted out to me to stay down whilst the other one shouted out 'man down'. It was funny looking back on it now, because I didn't realize they were talking about me. I wondered who *they were talking about at the time. I thought they were just pissing about.*

They both grabbed hold of me and started dragging me to safety and cover. I was in a bit of a daze as I'm sure you can imagine. It was only after the guys had taken off my body armour and then ripped open my T-shirt that I saw all of this blood. It was only then I realized that I had actually been shot and thought to myself, fucking hell. It was all very surreal because the battle was still going on around me and there was lots of incoming pinging about all over the place. I remember my boss asking me how I was and me telling him that I was fine and just to carry on and that there was no rush in getting me out of there. It makes me laugh looking back on it.

I was amazed at how calm he had been — not only throughout the actual incident itself but also now while he was recounting it to me.

When you realized that you had in fact been shot, how did you feel? *Instinctively you know it's not good, but you also know that it's not majorly bad either. It's not like I was coming round after being involved in a bomb blast, and having no feeling in either my arms or legs. I knew that I hadn't been hit in the arm, leg or chest where there are more veins arteries and organs, so I knew that it wasn't that serious. But at the same time you know you are out of the fight. I didn't know if the bullet had hit a bone or joint at that stage. Thankfully as it turned out it hadn't hit either. As we know, it had hit me quite high up and when it hit me I was actually leaning slightly forward, and also I instinctively ducked. I think that I was very lucky and I know that it could have been a lot worse for me.*

If the bullet had been even the slightest fraction lower, it would have shattered my collar bone into tiny pieces and could have sent the bullet tumbling off around my body, causing who knows what amount of damage.

And how did you feel about the medical treatment that you were given?

It was absolutely unbelievable. It was amazing watching all of that just slotting into place. My muckers on the ground bandaged me after tidying up the wound, which stopped it from bleeding too heavily. When I got casevaced out of there, there was a medic who made sure that I was all right. And when I got to Camp Bastion everybody was there just waiting for me. It was amazing really. If only the National Health Service was as quick and efficient as that, hey?

We both laughed. But Luke had been very lucky – and we were lucky to be here now, laughing together. The operation he was involved in saw the discovery and destruction of raw opium, numerous different guns and weapons, ammunition, RPGs and two suicide vests. A massive success by anyone's standards.

The answers I'd got from Ross and Luke were in many ways very different, highlighting their own individual characters and perspectives. I still wanted to know whether, overall, the sacrifices of British troops and the hardships they endure are worth it – which is the subject of the final chapter.

9

Why Are We There?

While my sons were deployed in Afghanistan, I decided to find out as much as I could about the country, its history and the reasons for the conflict, and try to discover whether the West's presence there is really justified. What follows is certainly not exhaustive, but just a record of my own thoughts and findings.

I started with a speech which Tony Blair gave in October 2001, where he outlined the apparent motives for the invasion. Here are some excerpts.

[. . .] No country lightly commits forces to military action and the inevitable risks involved but we made it clear following the attacks upon the United States on September 11th that we would take part in action once it was clear who was responsible.

There is no doubt in my mind, nor in the mind of anyone who has been through all the available evidence, including intelligence material, that these attacks were carried out by the al-Qaeda network masterminded by Osama Bin Laden. Equally it is clear that this network is harboured and supported by the Taliban regime inside Afghanistan.

It is now almost a month since the atrocity occurred, it is more than two weeks since an ultimatum was delivered to the Taliban to yield up the terrorists or face the consequences. It is clear beyond doubt that they will not do this. They were given the choice of siding with justice or siding with terror and they chose to side with terror.

There are three parts all equally important to the operation in which we're engaged: military, diplomatic and humanitarian. The military action we are taking will be targeted against places we know to be involved in the operation of terror or against the military apparatus of the Taliban. This military plan has been put together mindful of our determination to do all we humanly can to avoid civilian casualties.

I cannot disclose, obviously, how long this action will last but we will act with reason and resolve. We have set the objectives to eradicate Osama Bin Laden's network of terror and to take action against the Taliban regime that is sponsoring it. [...]

The world understands that whilst, of course, there are dangers in acting, the dangers of inaction are far, far greater: the threat of further such outrages, the threat to our economies, the threat to the stability of the world.

On the humanitarian front we are assembling a coalition of support for refugees in and outside of Afghanistan which is as vital as the military coalition. Even before September 11th, four million Afghans were on the move. There are two million refugees in Pakistan and one and a half million in Iran. We have to act for humanitarian reasons to alleviate the appalling suffering of the Afghan people and deliver stability so that people from that region stay in that region.

[...] I also want to say very directly to the British people why this matters so much directly to Britain. First let us not forget that the attacks of September 11th represented the worst terrorist outrage against British citizens in our history. The murder of British citizens, whether it happens overseas or not, is an attack upon Britain. But even if no British citizen had died it would be right to act.

This atrocity was an attack on us all, on people of all faiths and people of none. We know the al-Qaeda networks threaten Europe, including Britain, and, indeed, any nation throughout the world that does not share their fanatical views. So we have a direct interest in acting in our own self-defence to protect British lives. It was an attack not just on our lives but on livelihoods. We can see since 11th September how economic confidence has suffered with all that means for British jobs and British industry. Our prosperity and standard of living, therefore, require us to deal with this terrorist threat.

We act also because the al-Qaeda network and the Taliban regime are founded in large part on the drugs trade. Ninety per cent of all the heroin sold on British streets originates from Afghanistan. Stopping that trade is, again, directly in our interests.

I wish to say finally, as I've said many times before, that this is not a war with Islam. It angers me, as it angers the vast majority of Muslims, to hear Bin Laden and his associates described as Islamic terrorists. They are terrorists pure and simple. Islam is a peaceful and tolerant religion and the acts of these people are wholly contrary to the teachings of the Koran. [...]

This, of course, is a moment of the utmost gravity for the world. None of the leaders involved in this action want war. None of our nations want it. We are a peaceful people. But we know that sometimes to safeguard peace we have to fight. Britain has learnt that lesson many times in our history. We only do it if the cause is just; but this cause is just. The murder of almost several thousand innocent people in America was an attack on our freedom, our way of life, an attack on civilized values the world over. We waited so that those responsible could be yielded up by those shielding them. That offer was refused, we have now no choice so we will act. And our determination in acting is total. We will not let up or rest until our objectives are met in full. Thank you.

Tony Blair is good with words — very persuasive — but as I read further it did not seem to me that this was the whole story. Or if it was back in 2001, then perhaps the original reasons for our involvement were no longer holding good. To explore this I read up on Afghanistan's recent history.

The current situation in Afghanistan, of conflict and political instability, stems from the overthrow of King Zahir Shah in a coup back in 1973. King Shah was in Italy undergoing an eye operation at the time when he was ousted by his cousin, Mohammad Daoud, who then made himself president and turned Afghanistan into a republic.

In April 1978 there was a communist coup known as the April coup or the Saur, during which Mohammad Daoud and his entire family were shot dead.

Mohammad Daoud and Zahir Shah both descended from a family that had ruled the country for most of the past two hundred years. Now, instead, a Marxist government took over, led by Mohammad Taraki. The People's Democratic Party of Afghanistan (PDPA) was, however, riven by internal conflicts. Religious and ethnic rivalries and the landlocked, mountainous terrain (accounting for four-fifths of the country) have made it hard for the government in Kabul to rule effectively over their people. Mohammad Taraki had only been in power for 18 months when he was executed himself and the country's prime minister, Hafizullah Amin, seized power as the new president.

From the inner circles of the Kremlin, moves were afoot to get rid of him as well. The USSR saw him as an obstacle to a compliant communist government in Afghanistan. Amin was assassinated in December 1979, quickly followed by the Soviet Army's invasion of the country. A pro-communist puppet government was then put in place, led by a new president, Babrak Karmal, who had previously been the Afghanistan ambassador to the then communist country of Czechoslovakia.

The mujahideen Islamic fighters, including Osama Bin Laden amongst their number, were backed in their fight against the Soviet invaders and, it is said, armed, by none other than America. The Taliban grew strong during this time, supported surreptitiously by the US super-power that was using them to drive back the perceived communist threat.

In all, the Russians stayed in Afghanistan for the next ten years before they finally left it unceremoniously in 1989. Their stay was disastrous for the country in more ways than one. Millions of Afghans who were not prepared to bend to the will of the Soviets, and in effect become slaves in their own country, fled abroad to the safety of surrounding countries. Over a million Afghan citizens were killed by the Soviet Union's military intervention in their country.

The USSR's withdrawal of troops from Afghanistan came about in no small part because of the mujahideen's continuous attacks on the Soviet soldiers – who were frequently young, inexperienced recruits undergoing the equivalent of the USSR's national service. By the time the Soviets left Afghanistan there was a new president in charge of the country, President Najibullah, but he lasted only another three years. The country then became an Islamic Republic, whose new president was Professor Burhanuddin Rabbani.

When a Third World country suddenly rids itself of tyrannical foreign rulers, its new-found self-rule, and the power that comes with it, frequently brings its own problems. In Afghanistan the numerous mujahideen factions found it hard to agree amongst themselves about how best to run their newly independent and free country.

As a result of these divisions, thousands of Afghan citizens died at the hands of the mujahideen themselves. This took the country close to implosion. The Taliban originated from the south of the country, in particular from the city of Kandahar. As extreme Islamic fundamentalists, they brought with them another set of problems, governing with great severity and banning women's education. When they first came to power in 1994, they were supported by the majority of the country because of their promise to restore law and order and introduce a strict interpretation of Sharia law.

Osama Bin Laden and his group al-Qaeda claimed responsibility for the 9/11 attacks on the Twin Towers in New York City, and when the Taliban refused to hand him over, seeing him as a guest in their country, the US Government – alarmed at growing Islamic militancy in the country, and probably pursuing other self-interest agendas too — took this as an excuse to invade in October 2001. There has been a continuing foreign military presence in the country ever since, which led to a rout of the Taliban, though not to its final defeat. Recently, the Taliban has been gaining strength and support again, and making an increasingly vicious comeback. This is largely due to continuing chaos in the country and the presence of foreign troops. Many politicians in the West are now starting to speak of negotiating with this powerful force and trying to reach some accommodation with it, rather than simply crushing it — which has not so far worked and does not appear likely to at present.

The current government in Afghanistan, led by President Hamid Karzai, in effect only stays in power because of the support of American, UK and other allied forces. The ineffectiveness of the government to improve the lot of its people has allowed the Taliban to re-emerge as a major military power in the country.

President Karzai, from the southern city of Kandahar, is the country's first ever elected president, and regarded as a somewhat moderate and also weak leader, who has presided over continuing widespread corruption. He has political allies throughout the West and also the support — though recently also the criticism — of America. This support itself is something of a problem; he is disliked and mistrusted in certain circles throughout Afghanistan because of it. President Karzai has tried to secure international aid for his country. He continues his country's fight against drug trafficking, mainly in the rural areas, and has tried to improve the quality of his own security forces.

In December 2009 there were around 100,000 foreign troops in Afghanistan as part of the NATO International Security Assistance Force.

On the other side are the Taliban forces led by the religious cleric Mullah Omar.

The real irony here is that when Hamid Karzai first came to power he actually supported the Taliban and their aims. But after his father was murdered – a death they were blamed for – he changed his stance towards them.

Afghanistan is now one of the poorest countries in the world, left in ruins after decades of war and conflict. The government is effectively powerless outside the capital, Kabul. The rest of the country is under the control of numerous regional militia chiefs, or warlords, who are heavily involved in the drugs trade, both nationally and internationally. While the Taliban originally supported the cultivation of heroin, they subsequently banned it. Its cultivation nearly ceased altogether under their control, ironically increasing again to huge proportions after the American-led invasion, when the warlords became free to grow it again. Around 90 per cent of the world's heroin originates in Afghanistan – a hugely profitable crop for local warlords controlling the countryside, and a means of subsistence for ordinary people, providing them with food and basic requirements which they are unlikely to relinquish without a fight.

Even without the drugs trade in heroin, conflict in Afghanistan is endemic due to the many different ethnic and religious rivalries. Its population is composed of numerous different tribes: the Pashtuns make up 42 per cent of the population, followed by the Tajiks with 27 per cent and the Uzbeks and Hazaras both with 9 per cent each. There are also five other minor factions that collectively make up 12 per cent of the population. Each of these tribes has its own language and customs.

Only time will tell whether the West's invasion and subsequent occupation of Afghanistan has helped to improve the country in any way, or whether we are simply there for our own benefit, and have caused more chaos than good. Certainly the argument that Afghanistan is a hotbed of terrorism threatening Europe and therefore must be brought to heel seems flawed. There are grounds to believe that Pakistan is much more of a problem in this respect. And it may also be true that the West's presence in Afghanistan continues to act to turn it into a recruiting ground for terrorism. I am not convinced that the West can successfully impose its values, morals, culture and way of life on another country.

After this research and reading, I still did not feel I had my answer. Why *did* my sons, and other people's sons, have to risk their lives in this foreign country? September 11 was long past, and it seemed that perhaps we were simply embroiled in something we no longer knew how to extricate ourselves from. In February 2009 I therefore wrote the following letter to Gordon Brown, not sure if I would even get a reply:

Dear Prime Minister

As a nation we currently have a military involvement in Afghanistan, where we have been since October 2001; and it looks like we will be there for many more years to come.

Could I ask why our military involvement actually began in Afghanistan and what is the reason we are still there?

I ask this not as somebody who opposes the war but as the father of two sons who are currently serving in the British military. My younger son served as part of Herrick 8 and sustained a minor injury that saw him hospitalized at Camp Bastion. This resulted in his tour ending prematurely and his return to the UK.

My elder son is currently serving in Afghanistan as part of Herrick 9. In November 2008 he was involved in an incident where a suicide bomber, only a couple of feet away from him, pressed the detonator button on his bomb. The detonator exploded but thankfully the 70 lb of plastic explosive attached to the motorbike he was sitting on failed to go off. He was subsequently shot and wounded this month, resulting in his tour ending prematurely and his return to the UK.

My sons are soldiers. They do their duty and serve their country. That's as deep as they look at the situation in Afghanistan. They are simply doing their job.

I ask these questions because if either of them were to pay the ultimate price, as their father I would want to know what it was they had actually died for.

Yours sincerely
Stephen Wynn

I received my reply from Prime Minister Gordon Brown in April 2009. I must say that I was greatly impressed by his response: its honesty, clarity and frankness almost restored my faith in politics. But then I thought about the issues surrounding MPs and their expenses – and this trust simply evaporated again. (I have always drawn solace from the observations of the comic genius Billy Connolly, who once said, 'The desire to actually want to be a politician should bar you for life from ever being one!')

The letter was signed by Gordon Brown, though whether or not he actually wrote it I do not know. On the balance of probabilities it appeared to be genuine, which was of the utmost importance to me. I was also pleasantly surprised at the tone of his words.

8 April 2009

Dear Mr Wynn

Thank you for your letter dated 25 February about Afghanistan.

Firstly, let me begin by saying how proud we are of our Armed Forces, including your sons and all those who deploy on operations with them. I was sorry to hear of the injuries your sons sustained, particularly Luke who was shot while on operations near the town of Khan Neshin. I know that he and his fellow Marines from 42 Commando have been conducting operations in the southern-most regions of Helmand Province, defeating suicide bombers and engaging in fierce close-quarters combat to disrupt the enemy, and I salute their courage.

You have asked why we deployed to Afghanistan in 2001 and why we are still there. The answer is that our national security depends upon it. The attacks of 11 September 2001

1O DOWNING STREET
LONDON SW1A 2AA

THE PRIME MINISTER

8 April 2009

Dear Mr Wynn

Thank you for your letter dated 25 February about Afghanistan.

Firstly, let me begin by saying how proud we are of our Armed Forces, including your sons and all those who deploy on operations with them. I was sorry to learn of the injuries your sons sustained, particularly Luke who was shot while on operations near the town of Khan Neshin. I know that he and his fellow marines from 42 Commando have been conducting operations in the southern-most regions of Helmand Province, defeating suicide bombers and engaging in fierce close-quarters combat to disrupt the enemy, and I salute their courage.

You have asked me why we deployed to Afghanistan in 2001 and why we are still there. The answer is that our national security depends upon it. The attacks of 11 September 2001 were carried out by terrorists trained in Afghanistan and supported by the Taleban's sanctuary and assistance. Sixty-seven British citizens died in the attack on the World Trade Centre. Our own security is at risk if we allow Afghanistan to become again a safe haven for terrorists. It is for this reason above all that our Armed Forces are being asked to sacrifice so much on our behalf in Afghanistan.

This Government has always made it clear that it will keep the commitment of our Armed Forces in Afghanistan under review and, whilst we continue to make progress, it will take time and patience to achieve our objectives. I believe we must continue to be involved for the foreseeable future.

I hope this letter goes some way to addressing your concerns and I wish you and your sons well.

Yours sincerely

Mr Stephen Wynn

were carried out by terrorists trained in Afghanistan and supported by the Taleban's sanctuary and assistance. Sixty-seven British citizens died in the attack on the World Trade Centre. Our own security is at risk if we allow Afghanistan to become again a safe haven for terrorists. It is for this reason above all that our Armed Forces are being asked to sacrifice so much on our behalf in Afghanistan.

This Government has always made it clear that it will keep the commitment of our Armed Forces in Afghanistan under review and whilst we continue to make progress, it will take time and patience to achieve our objectives. I believe we must continue to be involved for the foreseeable future.

I hope this letter goes some way to addressing your concerns and I wish you and your sons well.

Yours sincerely
Gordon Brown

I was warmed by this letter, but ultimately this book is about Luke and Ross during their time serving in Afghanistan and how their experiences there have emotionally affected all three of us. I have no final answers to the question highlighted in this chapter, and must therefore leave it to the reader to decide whether the debt that has been paid in both death and injury during our involvement in Afghanistan has been worth it.

At the time of writing, in March 2010, a total of 278 British servicemen and women have been killed there since our first involvement in 2003, and 4960 have been wounded since 2008 alone (MOD figures).

Numerous reasons have been put forward as to why British troops are actually fighting in Afghanistan. They were supposedly sent there to assist and allow major reconstruction of the country to take place, to prevent the spread of terrorism to Europe, to try to suppress the influx of heroin into Britain, and to secure oil pipelines running through Afghanistan, carrying the much-needed fuel for our western economy. None of the first three, at least, have so far been achieved.

I am still not sure how the American and UK Governments ever thought they were going to change Afghanistan from a tribal society into a western-style democracy. Despite all the reasons and assurances I have been given about the need for our troops to be fighting this war, I remain unsure and ultimately unconvinced.

What I do know is that Ross and his mates will be back out serving their country once again in Afghanistan late in 2010, and that Luke will follow him out there in early 2011. I hope and pray that at the end of their tour they and their fellow soldiers will all return home fit and well to us, their families and loved ones. At present I'm trying not to think too much about how I will cope while my sons are out in Afghanistan again. One thing is certain: it doesn't get any easier.